HERITAGE

The Early English Barn
& The Kent Oasthouse

CHARLES A. MCARDELL

Published by CAMCA PUBLISHERS
11, Broadwater Gardens, Farnborough, Kent, BR6 7UQ.

Copyright © Charles A. Mcardell 2009

Reprinted with additional text and illustrations 2011

Charles A. Mcardell has asserted his moral rights
to be identified as the author

All rights reserved, No part of this book, text, photographs or drawings,
may be reproduced in any form or by any electronic or mechanical means,
including information storage or retrieval systems, without permission in writing
from the author in accordance with the provisions of the Copyright Act, 1956,
as amended by the Copyright, Designs and Patents Act, 1988.

A CIP Catalogue of this book is available from the British Library

ISBN 978-0-9562484-1-1

Cover design and typeset in Caslon 11pt
and Rotis Sans Serif
by Chandler Book Design,
www.chandlerbookdesign.co.uk

Printed in Great Britain by the
MPG Books Group, Bodmin and King's Lynn

PLATE 1 **Cressing Temple**
Roof Carpentry (Barley Barn)

PLATE 42: The Barley Barn
Roof Structure

C O N T E N T S

Chapter		Page
	Foreword	vii
	Acknowledgements	ix
	General Introduction	1
	List of Illustrations	5
One	Early English Barns	11
(i)	General survey of the changing agricultural scene, vanishing heritage, early English barns and their classification. Box frame, post and truss, cruck frame; structural form and carpentry.	13
(ii)	Perception of rural life in the later Middle Ages and the importance of the barn as a focus of rural activity.	37
(iii)	Population trends particularly from the 11th to the 16th centuries with some consequences for rural life.	51
(iv)	Medieval Building : Organisation and Techniques.	59
(v)	Annotated Barns Schedule	71
(vi)	Illustrated summaries of selected barns.	77
Two	An Introduction to Methods of Dating Timber Framed Barns	139
(i)	Historical Records - Parish records, estate maps and tithe maps.	141
(ii)	Radiocarbon C14 technique	145
(iii)	Dendrochronology Analysis	147

Three	The Kent Oasthouse	151
(i)	*The Buildings : Roundels and Square Kilns, Structure and Function*	156
(ii)	*Machinery and Equipment of the Period*	160

Four	Barns and Oasts : Brickwork and Decorative Features	203

Five	Planning and Legal Issues	217
(i)	The Problem of Redundant Farm Buildings, Conservation, Adaptive Re-use, Conversion	219
(ii)	Planning Constraints: legal considerations and law cases.	222

	Appendix A	231
	Appendix B	245
	Appendix C	249
	Appendix D	251
	Main References	255
	Bibliography	261
	Reflections	267
	Index	269

Foreword

This well illustrated book is presented in five distinct sections covering successively, the early English Barn with emphasis upon the medieval period including an overview of rural life in the later Middle Ages; information on population trends and building organisation and techniques; a technical section examining methods employed to determine the age of timber framed buildings particularly radio carbon (C 14) and dendrochronology dating. The third section considers Kent oasthouses of the 18th and 19th centuries with comment on machinery and equipment of the period; this is followed by a summary of the use of brick in early barns and oasts.

Finally a section on the planning, conservation and some legal issues to be considered when converting redundant farm buildings particularly for residential or community use.

The intention is to help stimulate interest in and appreciation of these splendid buildings including the history and craftsmanship embodied in them with the hope that some measure of the author's enthusiasm will be implanted in the readers and encourage them to pursue their interest by visiting the sites, supporting the conservation and restoration works and furthering their knowledge by recourse to the many detailed and technical publications now available some of which are referred to in the bibliography. These old farm buildings are as much a part of our cultural heritage as the more publicised stately homes, manor houses and large estates. Many would agree they deserve proper recognition.

Foreword to the Reprinted Edition 2011

The occasion of a book reprint provides the opportunity to introduce further text and illustrations. In particular, information is provided on the thirteenth century stone barn at Boxley Abbey in Kent and the fifteenth century timber framed barns of Faversham Abbey together with photographs of the buildings. Appendix B includes plans and cross section diagrams of each of the four Glastonbury Abbey barns. Appendix C contains a summary of the survey of traditional barns in England and Wales promoted and co-ordinated by the SPAB and at Appendix D examples of timber framing joints are illustrated by photographs and diagrams. Some additional text has been woven into other sections of the book in particular, planning changes and a law case which update and complement the original text.

Acknowledgements

Many people have assisted in the preparation of this book which draws upon research and work of a considerable number of authors many of whom are listed in the bibliography. Where extracts or quotes are used the author and book are identified in the text. I am indebted to them all. I am also grateful for the advice of officials at the many sites visited.

Particular thanks go to English Heritage for permitting the use of statistics and concepts set out in its joint publication with the Countryside Agency's Landscape, Access and Recreation Division and the University of Gloucestershire's Countryside and Community Research Unit. (See Bibliography).

My thanks also to the following:

Oxford University Press for consent to quote extracts from L.F. Salzman. East Sussex Records Office for advice concerning oasts at Flimwell (Ref. DUN - 42/3) Society for the Protection of Ancient Buildings for access to papers presented to the SPAB's Barns Conference in 1982.

My wife has been a source of regular encouragement throughout the long gestation period of this book and my thanks go to her for the support given particularly word processing the many draft manuscripts and editing. Technical computing support and photographic adjustments were provided by my son Kevin and my thanks also go to him.

I am indebted to Peter Bailey for his encouragement, guidance and advice on many barn issues and for undertaking the task of reading and commenting upon the draft manuscript.

Finally my thanks to the staff at Bromley Central Library for their help in tracing the many books and journals.

Photographs

Thanks to Peter Bailey for the photograph of Westenhanger barn prior to repair works and to Kevin for the photograph of Mote Farm Oast. All other photographs and drawings are the author's.

Acknowledgements for the Reprinted Edition 2011

My thanks to Robert Hale Ltd.., and the author Mr., R.J. Brown for their consent to reproduce the crown post roof diagrams contained in his book (Timber Framed Buildings of England) and The Boydell Press, Woodbridge and Mr. C.J. Bond and Mr. J.B. Weller for consent to reproduce plans and cross section diagrams of the four remaining Glastonbury Abbey barns as detailed in their essay on The Somerset Barns of Glastonbury Abbey which is part of the collection of essays in the book titled The Archaeology and History of Glastonbury Abbey.

My thanks also to Jennifer and Ian who provided pamphlets, background information and photographs of the Faversham barns in Kent.

My thanks especially to my wife Cora who has again provided support and encouragement as well as undertaking the task of deciphering my manuscript, editing and word processing. Thanks also to my son Kevin for providing the essential technical computing support including photographic modification.

General Introduction

The underlying motivation for the production of this illustrated book on Early English barns, in particular the medieval barn and Kent oast houses, derives from the author's long held keen interest in the subject and the desire to draw the attention of a wider audience to the beauty of these noble yet functional agricultural structures particularly at a time when the buildings are rapidly being lost either through dilapidation and vandalism or increasingly to conversion into residential properties. This latter is a highly controversial area both in planning terms and especially for the many preservation societies be they local trusts or national bodies.

When considering the medieval tithe barn or the monastic grange barn the grandeur of the structures, their sheer age and size, quality of the stonework, the intricacy of the timber framing, bulk of the posts and beams, complexity of roof joints, trusses, braces, rafters, collars and purlins clearly set them apart from all other forms of farm buildings. In history the threshing barn represents a focal point of unrelenting hard labour for the farm workers and a centre of accumulated wealth being a crop store for the landowner. The structures are a monument to the skill of the carpenter and the mason and have stood the test of time.

The care and maintenance of many of the best examples of the surviving barns, often listed properties, is now the responsibility of the National Trust, English Heritage or other local trusts but the dearth of grant money, the heavy cost of maintenance and repair coupled with the competition for individual project finance means sadly that worthy buildings will continue to deteriorate and may eventually be lost to posterity.

The second category of agricultural building reviewed is the oasthouse with its roundels or square kilns and the distinctive cowls revolving to the wind an agricultural building clearly associated with hop growing and the brewing industry. Indeed the largest complex of kilns and associated storage barns is that at the former Whitbread farm at Beltring, near Paddock Wood in Kent. This is illustrated and described in the third section of this book.

Once again it seems as agricultural incomes have eroded over time the need to raise finance has resulted in landowners selling off many of their former oast complexes now no longer needed for the hop industry as brewing techniques changed and with imported hops playing a more significant role. The oasts and barn structures readily convert to residential use to provide a distinctive type of dwelling that has captured the imagination of many. The author's survey of some three hundred oasts mostly in the Kent and Sussex area indicate a majority of the buildings are now in residential use, a few are used mostly for storage and still fewer are in traditional farm use and operate for the purpose for which they were built.

The book sets out particular information on types of barn structure including a commentary on some of the more common forms of timber framing, roof structures and jointing methods. For oasts, apart from a consideration of structure styles there is a brief summary of types of machinery and equipment associated with the hop drying process of the period.

This book confines itself to a general survey of two distinct forms of agricultural buildings - it does not purport to be a technically detailed treatise nor an advanced critique of existing understanding. Neither does it add to current knowledge on structures, dating techniques or chronology of building styles. It does however draw upon a wide range of significant learned and specialist published works in order to provide the reader in one place with a breadth and richly illustrated appreciation of the buildings and many related key issues. It attempts to stimulate and point the way forward for readers to develop their own particular areas of interest and to guide and help in pursuing those areas in greater depth and technical detail.

England's grand houses and large estates have for long received specific media focus and much has been written about them, their place in history and the lives of their illustrious occupants. This is rightly so, since they represent an important facet of our culture and heritage. However, this book is intended to divert the spotlight for a moment away from the grand and the comfortable by illuminating some of the more humble working buildings that well served the great estates and which provided essential employment for craftsmen and labourers throughout the late medieval period. The early English barn is a worthy subject in this endeavour.

The bibliography includes the many source books, pamphlets and documents from which this book has drawn and in which the diligent reader will find greater enlightenment.

List of Illustrations

1. Cressing Temple : Roof Carpentry (Barley Barn)
2. Littlebourne Barn : Vertical board cladding, brick plinth, passing brace half lapped to wall tie and rising to support the arcade post
3a. Scotney Castle Barn illustrating tie-beam over wall plate trenched into principal post
3b. Squinted lap joint - resists lateral withdrawal
3c. Purlin support to rafters
3d. Posts tenoned into mortices in groundsill on stone plinth
4. Bodium Castle : 1386
5. Carmelite Priory Gatehouse, Aylesford (15th century)
6. Carmelite Priory buildings with 13th century Pilgrims' Hall on extreme right
7. Avebury Barn - two side elevations
8. Avebury Barn - roof carpentry illustrating raking struts from tie-beam to principal rafter
9. Aylesford Carmelite Priory - north barn 18th century
10. Aylesford Carmelite Priory - roof carpentry of north barn showing queen posts
11. Aylesford Carmelite Priory - north barn post head joint and edge-halved scarf
12. Aylesford Carmelite Priory - 17th century west barn - two elevations
13. Bradford on Avon - north side elevation of tithe barn
14. Bradford on Avon - roof carpentry with raised base crucks
15. Bradford on Avon - view of upper cruck and collar beam with trenched purlins

16. Bradford on Avon - stone threshing floor
17. Doulting, Somerset - side elevation of stone barn
18. Glastonbury Abbey Tithe Barn - side elevation of barn
19. Glastonbury Abbey Tithe barn - decorative stonework to barn gable
20. Glastonbury Abbey Tithe Barn - roof carpentry illustrating the two tier cruck
21. Glastonbury Abbey Tithe Barn - arched wind braces
22. Great Coxwell Barn, Oxfordshire- side elevation of tithe barn
23. Great Coxwell Barn, Oxfordshire - central nave and roof carpentry
24. Great Coxwell Barn, Oxfordshire -principal posts, ties and wall plate
25. Great Coxwell Barn, Oxfordshire - gable end with 18th century door
26. Littlebourne Barn - side elevation
27. Littlebourne Barn - wagon door (framed, ledged and braced)
28. Littlebourne Barn - roof carpentry with crown post (two views)
29. St. Vincent's Church - 13th century adjacent to Littlebourne barn
30. Great Dixter - barn and oast kilns
31. Great Dixter - barn roof carpentry with king post
32. Coggeshall : The Grange Barn (1250)
33. Coggeshall : Crown Post Roof
34. Coggeshall Barn : Edge Halved Scarf Joint
35. Westenhanger Castle barns - hammer beam roof prior to repairs
36. Westenhanger Castle barn - gable end of the stable and storage barn
37. Westenhanger Castle barn -side view illustrating worked stone to door and windows (two views)
38. Westenhanger Castle barn - repaired arch braced hammer beam
39. Cressing Temple : The Wheat Barn (Two elevations)
40. Cressing Temple : The Wheat Barn Roof Structure
41. Cressing Temple : The Barley Barn (1200)
42. Cressing Temple : The Barley Barn Roof Structure
43. Frindsbury Barn, Rochester (1403)
44. Frindsbury Barn Crown Post Roof, Tie Beam, Post and Plate in "Normal" Assembly

45. Frindsbury Barn Wall Tie, Post and Plate in "Reversed" Assembly
46. Frindsbury Barn Stop Splayed Scarf Joint
47. Charing Archbishop's Palace Barn - the Great Hall (circa 1300) western elevation
48. Charing Archbishop's Palace Barn - roof structure with king posts (two views)
49. Exceat Barn, East Sussex - front elevation
50. Exceat Barn, East Sussex - side elevation of the building complex
51. Exceat Barn, East Sussex - roof carpentry
52. Dendrochronology - section through tree to expose growth rings
53. Humulus Lupulus : The Hop
54. Beltring Hop Farm : oasthouses on Bell Field (External kilns) (1880)
55. Beltring Hop Farm : two oasthouses in line on Bell Field (External kilns) (1880)
56. Beltring Hop Farm : Oasthouse (Internal Kilns) (1936)
57. Sissinghurst Castle Barn
58. Sissinghurst Castle Barn : roof carpentry with queen posts
59. Sissinghurst Castle : The Oasthouse , Brick Roundels and Square Kilns
60. Sissinghurst Castle : Opposite Elevation of the Kilns
61. Sissinghurst Castle : Base Fans to Roundels
62. Sissinghurst Castle : Rack and Pinion Hop Press
63. Sissinghurst Castle : Kiln Drying Floor - Slatted
64. Sissinghurst Castle : Beam Supports for Cowl Spindle within Cone Roof of Roundel
65. Sandling Farm: Museum of Kent Life: Oasthouse (Ragstone Roundels and Square Kiln) Two views
65(c) Sandling Farm Barn: Timber framed and weatherboarded
65(d) Sandling Farm Barn: Single hipped canopy cart entrance
65(e) Sandling Farm Barn: Internal view of aisled barn
66. Sandling Farm : Museum of Kent Life : Hop Pocket
67. Sandling Farm : hop barrow
68. Scotney Castle Estate : Timber Frame Barn

69. Scotney Castle Estate : Barn Queen Post Roof, Collar Beam with Clasped Purlin
69(b) Little Scotney Farm: Oasthouse with four roundels
69(c) Little Scotney Farm: Hop gardens
70. Chartwell : Kentish Ragstone Oasthouses (Residential Conversion) -two views
71. Spelmonden : Converted Brick Oasthouse (Office Conversion)
72. Mote Farm, Ightham : Kentish Ragstone Oasthouse - two views
72(c) Mote Farm: Ragstone barn with half-hipped clay tiled roof
73. Eden Farm, West Malling : Brick Oasthouse (Residential Conversion)
74. Eden Farm, West Malling : Exposed Rafters in Cone Roof of Roundel.
75. Eden Farm, West Malling : Kentish Ragstone Foundation to Roundel
76. Hadlow Maltings : Residential Conversion
77. Portman's Oast, Knockholt (Flint with Brick Banding)
78. Yonsea Farm, Woodchurch : Oasthouse
79. Yonsea Farm, Woodchurch : Granary with cart shed under (two views)
80. Goudhurst - Square kiln oasthouse - residential conversion
81. Brickwork : English Bond
82. Brickwork : Flemish Bond
83. Brickwork : English Garden Wall Bond
84. Brickwork : Header Bond
85. Brickwork : Stretcher Bond
86. Decorative Features : Dog Tooth at Eaves - West Malling
87. Decorative Features : Dog Tooth at Eaves - Spelmonden
88. Decorative Features : Dentil at Eaves - Beltring
89. Decorative Features : Diaper Pattern - Chapel Barn, Chiddingly
90. Decorative Features : Diaper Pattern - Shurland House
91. Decorative Features : Brick Noggin between close studding at Cressing Temple wheat barn
92. Brickwork - Lime Staining

Appendix A

93   Boxley Abbey Barn: South side elevation of stone barn

94   Boxley Abbey Barn: North side elevation looking to the west
95   Boxley Abbey Barn: North side elevation looking to the east
96   Boxley Abbey Barn: West gable end
97   Boxley Abbey Barn: Scissor truss roof
98   Boxley Abbey Barn: Scissor truss roof
99   Boxley Abbey Barn: King posts
100 Faversham Abbey Farm Barns, Kent: Major and Minor Barns
101(a) Major Barn: Timber framed and aisled (15th century)
101(b) Major Barn: Principal posts, tie beams and plate in normal assembly with arch bracing
102 Minor Barn Timber framed and aisled (15th century)
103 Minor Barn: Unshaped principal post
104 The King's Warehouse: Octagonal crown post with head bracing (two views)
105(a) The King's Warehouse: Timber framed (15th century)
105(b) The King's Warehouse : Plain crown post supported by arch bracing from the tie beam

Appendix B
106 Glastonbury Abbey Barns: Outline plans of the four barns with cross sections of each

Appendix D
107(a) Notched collar beam clasping purlin to rafter with queen post support
107(b) Queen strut from tie beam clasps purlin to rafter - no collar beam
108   Stop splayed scarf joint - extends wall plate
109   Oak dowels secure rafters at the apex of porch roof
110   Solid knee brace from post to bridging beam into which the joists are set
111   Sussex cowl : flat top (cap) similar to the Kent cowl but with a reduced and hooded opening
112   Diagrams of crown post roofs

Line Drawing
Post and Truss Aisled Barn

CHAPTER 1

Early English Barns

1 (i)   A Vanishing Heritage

Existing farm buildings reflect in their location, structural form and building style the significant changes that have taken place in English agriculture, the countryside and rural life over the past one thousand years. The structures are valuable assets. They represent an important facet of the national heritage and contribute to the understanding and appreciation of our rural history.

English Heritage in its recent publication "Living Buildings in a Living Landscape" has focused upon traditional farm buildings and identifies some distinctive attributes which are reproduced below :

- Traditional farm buildings make a major contribution to the character of English landscape. They hand down messages from the past telling us how our ancestors farmed, lived, thought and built.

- They represent an historical investment in materials and energy that can be sustained through conservation and careful re-use and are crucial to our understanding of settlement patterns and the development of today's countryside being irreplaceable repositories of local crafts, skills and techniques in harmony with their surroundings. They provide an important economic asset for farm businesses or, through adaptive re-use when they have become redundant, a high quality environment for new rural businesses.

Clearly these farm assets are valued in terms of cultural history and heritage. Sadly their continued availability is not guaranteed.

Despite the endeavours of the many preservation societies and national institutions such as English Heritage, the National Trust and the work of the Society for the Protection of Ancient Buildings, many barns and other farm buildings continue to fall into decay and collapse, whilst others are sold off for conversion for non - traditional uses. Protection provided by the planning laws, listed building controls, development controls, local conservation area restrictions, building regulations, etc., each operate to put a brake upon the waste of these valued structures. Nevertheless a significant reduction in traditional farm buildings continues to take place. The pool of quality inevitably declines and with it comes the dilution of heritage. We need to consider why the buildings that for hundreds of years have been a vital farming resource have now become almost a liability for the particular landowners on whose acreage they stand. The enormous changes in the nature of farming particularly the increases in mechanisation in the 19th and 20th century, the drive for greater units leading to farm mergers, the decline in farm profitability are some of the forces of change which make traditional historic structures inadequate to cope with new demands.

Old barns become incapable of housing the new agricultural machinery, the giant tractors and combine harvester which literally could not manoeuvre through the largest of porches or between the arcade posts of aisled barns, hence the new metal and concrete vast hangar like barn structures that erupted over many of the large arable holdings. The lack of, or inadequacy of grant aid to help maintain the older redundant historic barns or to provide for derelict building repairs coupled with declining farm profits inevitably contributed to the deterioration over time of the old barn. The attractiveness to the farmer of a capital receipt if the structure could be sold off for re-development or residential use is quite apparent. Development controls and other planning constraints might prevent inappropriate re-use but could not obviate eventual decay and collapse of the unused structure or its destruction by vandalism and fire. Readers will no doubt be aware of the serious fire damage occasioned to old buildings generally. An unused, isolated old barn is a sitting target.

The challenge is how to facilitate adaptive re-use of farm buildings as a means of promoting rural diversification and regeneration through innovative schemes that create local employment, i.e. farm shops, craft workshops, small business units, small industrial units or failing all else use for storage. Such uses retain the outward appearance of the barn for posterity, bring the building back to life, and provide employment through economic use. Internally, sub-division without loss of the exposure of roof trusses, beams and bracing protects the quality of original craftsmanship and enables it to be available to view. Many examples exist where historic barns have been rescued for posterity by creative re-use; the barn at Avebury is now a museum of rural life, the Glastonbury barn similarly. At Old Basing the restoration of the 16th century brick barn has produced a valuable community asset, the flint barn at Exceat (West Dean) now operates as the centre for the Seven Sisters Country Park. Other barns of quality have been rescued by English Heritage, the National Trust and local preservation societies and remain open to interested visitors, societies and tourists. The high quality of these listed structures demands they be preserved at public expense despite no viable alternative use being found to finance their maintenance or to make them economically productive.

The following statistics demonstrate some of the key factors affecting farming in Britain today.

Data Source

DEFRA 2005	In the decade between 1995 and 2005 the total income from farming fell in real terms by 60%.
	Cost of farm inputs : land, labour, fertilizers, machinery have increased more than the product prices and compliance with improved animal welfare regulations, traceability, food safety, etc. imposes increased costs. The reduction in farm subsidies and the re-categorisation of grant purposes has also impacted adversely on farm incomes exacerbated by the operation of the Common Agricultural policy.

DEFRA 2004	Farm Practices Survey
	One in five farms have redundant traditional farm buildings (excludes farms without traditional buildings). Similarly 25% of such farms have traditional buildings in disrepair, a significant proportion are claimed to be in an advanced state of structural decay including 7% of all principal listed structures (Grade I and II Star).
Gaskell and Clark 2005 (English Heritage)	For the period 1980 - 2001 over half of all listed farm buildings have been subject to planning applications for development. 31% of listed farm buildings have been converted to other uses. Farmers have liquidised assets to pay off debts, buy additional land or convert buildings for renting.

Early English Barns and Their Classification

Having set out a summary of some aspects of the agricultural dilemma leading to the decline in number and redundancy of many traditional farm buildings we need to move on to the main theme of this book, in particular an appreciation of the early English barns with emphasis upon those constructed in the later Middle Ages, their structural form and classification. An illustrated analysis of structural features and carpentry is followed by a brief summary of rural life in the 11th to 16th centuries setting the early barn, its place, importance and use, in the context of the essentially feudal agricultural economy of the period. The Oxford English Dictionary provides a useful starting point to distinguish the nature of the term monastic grange barn from the ecclesiastical tithe barn. It is well accepted however that over time any large barn was usually called a tithe barn whatever its principal purpose since many monasteries as well as the parish church had authority to collect tithes.

Monastic Grange – Barn

An establishment where farming is carried on. A farmhouse, a repository for grain, a granary, a barn. The grange barn stored the harvested corn prior to winter threshing to yield the grain. In practice, the grange barns would have stored all the produce of the monastery's lands that were to support the monastic community including the numerous lay brothers and where the monasteries owned parishes then the tithe would also require to be stored.

Tithe Barn

The tithe barn known as the vicars' barn wherein was stored the tenth part of the annual produce of agriculture etc., being a due or payment (tax) on produce (later in cash/produce) charged on the parish for the support of the priesthood, the upkeep of the church and to provide for the poor of the parish. Tithe barns were invariably located near to the parish church.

How may we effectively classify the great diversity of early English barn styles be they monastic granges, tithe barns, field barns, threshing barns, barns for general storage of grain, or for livestock? A simple categorisation could be by purpose, alternatively by visual appearance thereby simply differentiating by type of building e.g. timber structure, stone structure, brick or flint structure with roof coverings of clay tile, stone tile, straw or reed thatch. However the superficial nature of these general classifications provides little help in understanding the true nature of the barn , and no appreciation of the considerable skilled craftsmanship embodied within the building. The general consensus looks therefore to the manner in which barns were built, specifically the way the enormous stresses of compression, tension, racking, shearing, twisting, are withstood and controlled by the structure in particular the methods by which the massive weight of the roof is safely transferred to the ground. It seems readily apparent this latter approach is the classification that most clearly demonstrates and differentiates the nature of barns from one another and how they work in coping with the massive forces exerted upon them by the roof timbers, the tiles and the effects of the elements particularly wind pressures, snow and rain. The approach presents us with three distinct types of structure but there are many variations within each category.

Box Frame Structures

The walls are the basic structure. There is an absence of internal vertical load - bearing timbers which has the advantage of leaving the internal space uncluttered. The stone, flint or brick walls have to be thick enough to resist the crushing weight of the roof and the walls will normally be heavily buttressed to resist the outward pressures exerted by the roof. Examples are found at Hales (Norfolk), Abbotsbury (Dorset) and Sissinghurst Kent.

Post and Truss Structures

These timber framed buildings are distinguished from the box frame structure by having the full weight of the roof carried on the vertical timber posts and not the barn walls. The presence of a row of vertical arcade posts with the extension of the roof rafters to the outer side of the arcade plate creates an aisle which may extend along one elevation or both sides, or even all round the structure (refer to line drawing). The divisions between the pairs of vertical posts creates bays and it is by the number of bays we normally describe the size of the barn .Horizontal tie beams are fixed transversely across the width of the barn to connect the pairs of principal posts and principal rafters thereby pulling the frame together in order to counteract the considerable outward thrust exerted by the weight of the roof. At a higher level collar beams join pairs of principal rafters to further secure the frame which is again strengthened by purlins running the length of the roof and providing support to the common rafters. The triangulation of the truss configuration provides considerable strength and rigidity to the frame. It is normal to have bracing timbers tenoned into mortices on each side of the principal posts and tenoned again in mortices cut into the arcade plate. Similarly a brace from the principal post into the tie-beam. The base of the principal posts would be tenoned into a massive sill beam which may be elevated on a stone or brick plinth to obviate potential rot and to spread the load. Enclosure of the timber framed structure may be achieved by timber cladding. In early barns the boarding would be of vertical planks as at Frindsbury and Littlebourne in Kent. (Plate 2). Later horizontal weatherboarding becomes more common. Alternative materials would be stone walls, flint or brick. At Cressing Temple the wheat barn has

PLATE 2: Littlebourne Barn
Vertical board cladding, brick plinth, passing brace half lapped to wall tie and rising to support the arcade post

brick infill between the close studding. The consistent factor is that load bearing remains onto the principal posts and through them to the ground. The structural features set out in this description are well illustrated at Cressing Temple by the Wheat Barn and Barley Barn.

Cruck Frame Structure

The cruck frame is formed from a pair of inward curving timbers (blades), each pair often derived from a single tree trunk or large curved branch cleaved down the middle to create a matching pair of curved timbers. The cruck blades are secured together by a lapped transverse tie-beam. A collar beam or yoke would be fixed (lapped) higher up the cruck blade for additional strength, and a series of these cruck frames are sequentially reared to the vertical and joined longitudinally by a heavy ridge purlin to provide essential rigidity. The horizontal wall plate sits on top of the extended tie beam on the outer side of the blades and together with purlins trenched into the blades would secure and support the rafters and stabilise the structure. By virtue of their physical shape the curved cruck blades operate as structural posts and as the principal roof rafters. The full weight of the roof presses directly upon the wall plate, purlins and cruck blades. The latter, which carry the wall plate and purlins transfer the total weight down through the substantial blade timbers onto the ground. The base of the cruck timbers normally stand upon stone or lime cement pads or even layers of large pebbles rammed into the soil. This protective base not only helps prevent ground water being sucked up into the end grain of the timber thereby reducing potential rot, but acts to spread the transferred roof weight over a wider ground area. In addition to the full cruck frame described above, there are a number of variations including the "raised cruck" where the feet of the cruck blades rise up from supporting solid walls e.g. the Bradford on Avon barn. In other forms the main tie-beam (closed form) may be omitted to create more usable space, but is replaced with cruck spurs from the blades tying them to the wall plate and vertical wall posts.

Elements of Structure and Carpentry

A meaningful appreciation of the construction skills involved in building a timber framed barn requires careful examination of specific barn buildings at close range. Readers are urged to select and visit the best examples of the preserved barns many of which are under National Trust stewardship and readily accessible. A guide to some of the key features to look for include the following which sets out information on roof forms, construction methods including carpentry joints and specific barn features and terminology. It is in their roof carpentry that the large older barns come most closely to the beauty that is so evident in many of our cathedral churches. The massive size of the barn timbers, the complexity of the jointing, the configuration of the bracing and strutting, the truss triangulation each of these demand close examination in order to appreciate the skill of the early craftsmen. Four main forms of roof structure to look for are the King Post, Queen Post, the Crown Post and the Hammerbeam roof.

The most prevalent form of barn roof in the south east of England from the 13th century was the Crown Post in which a single timber post framed into the transverse tie-beam rises vertically to support the collar beam purlin and is footbraced either side from the tie-beam. The Crown Post which is under compression secures and supports the collar purlin and may be headbraced to it on one or each side. See examples at Littlebourne Barn and Frindsbury barn .

The King Post is a vertical timber post rising from the centre of the tie-beam to the ridge beam, this latter being a horizontal beam at the apex (arris) of the roof running the length of the barn and securing the tops of the rafters. Ridge beams provide longitudinal stability but were not common in South East England until the mid 18th century. Refer to Great Dixter and note the metal fixing to the underside of the tie beam that secures the pendant King Post which is under tension.

The Hammerbeam roof is well illustrated at Westenhanger barns. The principle here was to unclutter the "nave" of the barn by doing away with the full arcade posts. The remaining upper part of the vertical (hammer) posts rises to the transverse collar or straining beam and sits upon the truncated hammerbeams which are themselves supported by heavy curved braces (brackets) anchored into the three foot thick

Kentish ragstone walls. The feet of the bracing posts are supported upon stone corbels set into the walls well above head height.

The Queen post roof is distinguished by two upright posts rising from the tie-beam and jointed by tenons into mortices cut into the underside of the collar beam and secured by dowels. In some instances the lap joint is used. Refer to Aylesford Priory Barn and Scotney Castle barn .

Roofing materials in the early barns were of long straw thatch or where available the more expensive but more durable water reed thatch. In areas where stone tiles were available they would be used but being considerably heavier than thatch required stronger roof timbers and additional bracing to carry the weight. Clay peg tiles became widely used throughout the later middle ages. Littlebourne Barn is reed thatch Frindsbury is clay peg tile and Great Coxwell stone tile .

Carpentry Joints

The more common carpentry joints in use in the 13th century in timber frame construction included variations of the lap joint particularly used for crossing timbers providing bracing e.g. the passing brace running from the aisle stud and halved across the principal post to the tie beam. An improved form of this joint was the notched lap which resisted withdrawal. Mortice and tenon joints have a long history and are the main joint used to secure the principal posts into the groundsill beam. The heavy tie beams are jointed with mortices onto tenons cut into the thick jowl heads of the principal posts. Collar beams are tenoned at each end to insert into mortices cut into the pairs of principal rafters (alternatively lap jointed). The feet of the principal rafters are stub tenoned into mortices cut into the upper surface of the tie-beam. Crown posts and King posts are tenoned into a mortice cut into the upper face of the tie beam Bracing timbers may also be tenoned into the beam mortices with the other end tenoned into mortices cut into the side of the Crown Post or King Post.

Scarf joints were used to extend the main horizontal timbers such as wall plates, arcade plates and purlins. Since many early barns are well in excess of 100 ft. in length, many being 150-200 ft., three or four pieces of heavy timber needed to be jointed together end to

Early English Barns | 23

PLATE 3a: **Scotney Castle Barn**
Illustrating tie-beam over wall plate trenched into principal post

PLATE 3b
Squinted lap joint - resists lateral withdrawal

end to form the full sized plates or purlins. The nature and efficiency of the scarf joint developed over time but an excellent example of an early form of stop splayed scarf is illustrated at Frindsbury. A second type of scarf (edge halved) is shown at Coggeshall.

Joints were secured by oak dowels driven into holes drilled through the timbers pinning the tenon into the mortice and thereby resisting withdrawal. The demonstration of precision techniques in jointing is well illustrated by the practice of drilling mortice and tenon dowel peg holes slightly out of alignment with the consequence that when the joint was assembled and dowel pegs driven home the tenon was forced more tightly into the mortice. Where timbers were re-used (and recycling seemed common) joints may have required alternative treatment to ensure a secure fit and wedges might be driven into the tenon end to tighten it in the re-used mortice.

A complex and sophisticated joint was the posthead lap dovetail. This was used in the framing of the tie-beam over the jowl post to which it was secured by mortice and tenon, and over the wall plate using a lap dovetail joint to resist lateral withdrawal. The wall plate is trenched into the top of the jowl post and secured by mortice and tenon to it i.e. the wall plate is effectively sandwiched between jowl post and tie-beam. This is termed "normal" assembly (plate 3a). Roof purlins set at the roof angle are trenched or notched into the principal rafters.

By the 13th century the post in hole or earth foot construction approach to timber framing with its pronounced tendency for posts to rot due to exposing the raw end of the principal timbers directly to ground moisture had given way to the heavy ground sill beam lying horizontally upon rammed soil or elevated above the ground onto low stone, flint or later brick walls. This latter method had the additional advantage of enabling levels to be more easily established. Foundations were of rammed stone, chalk or flint even timber piling of soft ground was practiced but not as far as I am aware when building timber framed barns. Principal arcade posts stood upon stone or lime mortar pads. This not only helped prevent post end rot but spread the loads over a wider ground area. In some barns the arcade posts were tenoned into a short sill spur extending inwards from the main ground sill.

Early English Barns | 25

PLATE 3c
Purlin support to rafters

PLATE 3d
Posts tenoned into mortices in groundsill on stone plinth

Mechanics of the Frame

The carpenters' skills embraced not only a deep practical understanding of the nature and strength of particular timbers for use as structural posts or plates in particular the qualities of the oak, the elm, chestnut, ash, etc. and a sound practical knowledge of cutting, shaping and jointing large timbers but essential was a knowledge of geometry and of mechanics. The carpenter had to evaluate the probable ways the great weight of the barn roof would impact upon its supporting members, what stresses of compression or crushing forces, extension, shearing, probabilities of racking and flexing would be encountered not only from the weight of the structure but also those imposed by the vagaries of weather. The task was to develop a frame of sufficient strength and bracing to resist these potentially destructive forces. In practice, many of the early barns have stood the test of time and show a resilience perhaps not generally seen in more modern structures. Clearly the master carpenters and journeymen were expert at their craft and in current parlance we perhaps would say the structures were over engineered to include a useful margin of safety. An interesting structural analysis to illustrate this point is found in the guide pamphlet for the tithe barn of the Augustinian Priory of St. Mary's, Carlisle. Dated to the late 15th century the barn measures 115ft. by 27 ft. its walls are of coursed red sandstone some 3ft. 7 ins. thick and the oak tie beams 30ft. long x 1ft. 9 ins thick. The principal upright timber posts on the open north side of the barn are 20 ins. x 15 ins. in section but during restoration work in 1969 a structural analysis proved an adequate and safe size to carry the roof weight and associated stresses would by 9 ins. x 9 ins., precautionary in the extreme!

When we refer to the mechanics of the structural frame we must be aware of the laws of physics, in particular we consider the forces and stresses that may be imposed upon it and the way in which each of these can be calculated in order to determine the thickness of timber required and strutting, bracing and jointing essential to resist these forces and ensure the frame remains functional and sound. The mathematics and formulae involved is outside the scope of this book but the following general summary should suffice to generate in the interested reader a desire to pursue the science in more detail. (Refer to J. Newlands "The

Carpenters' Assistant"). We can postulate that an expression of the mechanics of the timber frame is reflected in its structural form, namely, the substantial nature of its principal posts, tie beams, principal rafters and purlins, the sill beams and wall plates together with its roof truss triangulation with bracing and strutting designed to strengthen and stiffen the frame and jointing methods crafted to resist withdrawal or tearing apart of the joined timbers. The destructive forces that need to be considered include :

Extension

This is a force acting in the direction of timber fibres trying to tear them apart by stretching motion. It affects the transverse tie beams due to the outward thrust of the principal roof rafters as they attempt under the force of the roof weight and gravity to stretch the beam at each of its ends.

Compression

A crushing force acting in the direction of the timber fibres. The principal posts are subject to this force as the weight of the roof is conveyed down through them to the sill beam or barn floor padstone. The collar beam also suffers compression where it acts to prevent rafters sagging inwards.

The principal rafters are also under compression since the roof weight presses down upon them yet they cannot move since their feet are held firm by the tie beam. Mr. Hewett in his "English Historic Carpentry" comments the majority of brace timbers were designed to act in compression, e.g. the wind brace, wall brace and shore.

Torsion

This twisting force operates to split and tear the timber fibres apart. We can envisage this affecting the barn roof when it is under severe strain from fierce wind pressures resulting in twisting of the rafters as the roof yields by racking to one end. The collar purlin and side purlins strengthened by wind braces between purlins and principal rafters were developed to help obviate this problem. The hipped roof offers greater resistance to racking than the gable end. The circa 1500 Grade 11* six bay cruck barn at Court Farm, Aylton in Herefordshire currently under repairs with a Natural England/English Heritage grant has a frame that leans some two metres from the vertical. The cruck blades have twisted under torsion but have not yet sheared. (SPAB Cornerstone 2007).

Right-angled pressure

Pressures at right-angles to the direction of the wood fibres seek to rupture the timber. A Crown Post supporting a collar purlin exerts such a downward force on the tie beam. The King Post roof is quite different. The principal rafters are jointed into the top of the King Post and since they are unable to push outwards at their lower ends because they are framed firmly into the tie-beam the top of the King Post becomes a fixed point and the post acts as a pendant. Any tendency for the tie-beam to sag along its length under its own weight is resisted by the framing of the bottom of the King Post into the beam and consequently the King Post will, under such circumstances, be under tension.

It is the effective triangulation of the pair of principal rafters, tie-beam and King post that keeps the truss rigid. Bracing from the principal posts to the underside of the tie beam acting in compression also help prevent the beam sagging. Similarly, bracing from tie beam or base of King Post to each of the pair of principal rafters resists inward sag of the rafters. Mr. C. Hewett details examples of the King Post acting as pendant (under tension) at the Tower of London Council Chamber roof where it helps support the side purlins and to resist sagging of the tie beam, and alternatively acting under compression at the Great Hall roof of Staple Inn at High Holborn He further comments it was during the 18th century that suspended King Posts with iron footstraps first appeared and quotes a dated example from 1750 in a barn at Felsted, Essex. Queen Posts may similarly operate in compression or tension. In the latter instance where the two vertical posts are framed into a straining beam set between two principal rafters they operate as pendants and being also framed into the tie beam help resist any tendency of that beam to sag. The straining beam will be under compression as it prevents the rafters sagging inwards, the Queen Posts will be under tension, the rafters under compression and the tie-beam under tension. Mr. Hewett provides the example of Tewksbury Abbey where Queen Posts are lap dove-tailed to the collar beam and tie-beam and are in tension. With the clasped purlin roof form a collar beam traps and secures the purlin to the principal rafter and is supported by Queen Posts acting in compression. In some structures the collar beam may be absent and two raking struts rise from the tie beam and directly clasp the purlins to the principal rafters. In such a frame the struts act in compression.

Controlled laboratory tests have been undertaken over many years on a range of timbers to assess their strength and elasticity i.e. their ability to return to their normal condition subject to withdrawal of a given force. Similarly, other tests have included application of tension, compression, torsion and rightangled forces to calculate for a given volume, or length of, timber, its actual point of failure. Formulae have been developed indicating the crushing force for any given timber i.e. the point at which it will be unable to resist the given weight and therefore will fail. Similarly for each of the forces encountered. However the skills and knowledge of the medieval carpenter including his ability to make these essential judgements in the absence of sophisticated laboratory testing clearly developed over time with the passing down of craft experience including lessons learned from the inevitable failures of some structures from time to time. The archives record many such failures.

Dr. Bronowski (The Ascent of Man) comments upon Greek and Roman structures particularly the nature of stresses in stone, essentially forces of compression, but his specific references to the horizontal beam are relevant to the tie-beam within a timber-framed barn. In summary, the proposition is where a beam is placed horizontally connecting the tops of two vertical posts, stresses within that beam will increase the further the supporting posts are apart since the longer the unsupported length of beam the greater will be the compression its weight produces in the upper layers of its wood fibres and the greater the tension (stretching) produced in fibres of the lower, underside, of the horizontal beam at its centre, as it begins to sag. An effective form of bracing is essential since the beam could split or fail completely or flex and destroy the integrity of the truss. Such flexure could prove disastrous to the whole frame.

Barn Features and Terminology

Much has already been said concerning various forms of barn structure in the earlier sections of this book but interesting visual features to be observed and considered when visiting specific barn sites are set out below.

Roof Designs

Distinguish the gable end roof as illustrated at Great Coxwell and contrast it with the hipped roof at Frindsbury and the half-hipped roof at one end of the Exceat barn. The gablet roof style comprising a hipped roof into which, near the ridge, a small gable is set is seen at Cressing Temple wheat barn . Internally, the nature of barn roof structures and triangulation of timbers has already been commented upon but identify whether these are Crown Post, King Post (pendant), Queen Post (under tension or compression) or Hammerbeam. Look particularly at the truss configuration and bracing, in particular whether there are passing or scissor braces. Are the carpentry joints secured with dowel pegs supplemented by more recent metal strap work. Evidence of recycling of old timbers will be seen at most early English barns since due to their age they will have experienced much change, replacement parts and maintenance. The presence of over-sized mortices, unfilled mortices, unfilled lap joints and empty peg holes is clear evidence of re-use.

A classification of roof forms is a major study in itself since Mr. R. A. Cordingley in his "British Historical Roof Types and their Members" defines eight major groups and seventy five classifications within these groups. It is outside the scope of this book but readers may wish to pursue their interests further.

Thatch

Early forms of roof coverings to keep out the wind and rain from a building were types of "thack", being heather, bracken, straw or reed. Hay was inadequate since it quickly absorbed moisture and was subject to rapid rotting. The early medieval barns would probably have been covered with wheat straw or water reed, if locally available.

Long straw required collecting into manageable bunches with the grain shaken out to prevent green growth and combed with a thatching fork to make the straws parallel. These bunches, called yelms, were fastened with straw ropes and the thatcher would lay them onto the rafters and laths commencing at the eaves and working upwards towards the ridge with a good overlap of each top bundle over the lower. The bundles were secured in position by straw ropes passed across the horizontal layers and tied to the rafters by means of large hazel staples or rods hammered by mallet into the straw and secured on the inner side to the laths and rafters. This process remains virtually unchanged today. The ridge posed a particular problem since water reed was inflexible and could not be bent across the ridge. However long straw could be moulded over the ridge or turves could be used. Sometimes a clay covering would be used.

Salzman records the following comparative costs in Ripon in 1392.

- 160 thraves of barley straw for thatching at a halfpenny cost six shillings and eight pence.
- 20 thraves of rye straw for thatching cost two shillings.
- 22 thraves of wheat straw cost two shillings and nine pence.

He concludes that it would seem wheat straw was regarded as the best for the purpose since it commanded the higher price (Note - twelve pence equals one shilling and twenty shillings equals one pound).

The Barn Porch

Many barns lack a protective porch entrance the great doors being set directly into the side elevation of the framework. Some have a protruding canopy. However, wagon porches did play an important protective role since they offered shelter from adverse weather to the horse-drawn wagons piled high with their harvested sheaves of corn when they arrived and waited to be unloaded into the threshing barn. Entrance porch doors are generally much higher than exit doors situated on the opposite side of the barn since by the time the wagon was ready to leave it had been unloaded and the head room required was considerably reduced. Porches come in various styles in particular see the two thatched canopy porches at Littlebourne barn and contrast them with the two hipped and clay peg-tiled timber clad porches at Coggeshall. The brick barn at Sissinghurst lacks a porch and the barley barn at Cressing Temple boasts a large single centrally situated porch. At Glastonbury we see a massive stone buttressed porch and at Bradford on Avon two large stone porches.

Threshing Floor

The threshing floor is sited across the barn between entrance and exit doors. The floor comprised hard rammed clay or chalk or sometimes was stone flagged . Records indicate that at some barns one of the large doors would be removed and laid upon the ground to act as a threshing floor. Hand threshing by flail was an arduous lengthy and chokingly back breaking dirty labour lasting many winter days and similarly the winnowing process to separate chaff from grain This was the lot of the peasant farm worker in the later Middle Ages. It would have been no easier in other occupations available to the peasantry.

Barn Alignment

Consider the manner in which the barn is aligned in the context of the prevailing weather. A supposition is the doors should be exposed to the prevailing winds such that as the corn was threshed and winnowed the breezes would operate to carry away from the grain the separated chaff and dust caused by the threshing. A plank fixed across the bottom of the doorway acted to prevent the grain, being heavier than the chaff from also being blown away as the winnowing progressed. This arguably gives rise to the concept "the threshold" of a dwelling. .

Bays and Trusses

The nature of timber framing provides divisions within the barn termed bays and these are typical of post and truss structures which are common in the south-east of England. The wall bays are formed by the positioning of the arcade posts and an average distance between such principles would be some fifteen feet. The distance between two sets of triangulated roof trusses is termed the roof bay. It is a common practice to refer to the size of a barn by the number of wall bays it has e.g. a five bay barn or a seven bay barn. In approximating the barn length an allowance has to be added for the two end aisles (if they are present) together with the entrance door areas which may be wider or less than a standard bay.

Terminology

Arcade Post

A principal post vertically positioned separating the central nave from the side aisle. The arcade post supports the arcade plate which is a heavy horizontal timber running the length of the barn and securing the tops of several arcade posts. The plate supports the rafters. The arcade posts carry the full weight of the barn roof and transfer it to the ground either to a sill beam or padstone each of which spread the transferred load. Thickening at the top of the post is termed a jowl.

Brace

A diagonal timber which acts under compression to strengthen the barn frame. Braces may be straight or curved and feature particularly in the post and truss barn where they act to strengthen the arcade plate being tenoned into the principal post and into the underside of the plate. Bracing of the Crown Post to the tie-beam or collar is normal. Bracing between wall studs is also common.

Collar Beam

A horizontal timber set transverse the barn to secure two principal rafters. It acts under compression to prevent the rafters sagging. The collar beam is situated above the tie-beam.

Purlin

A horizontal timber running the length of the barn roof notched or trenched into the principal rafters and giving support to the common rafters. It provides a resistance to the potential for racking.

A Collar Purlin

A horizontal timber carried by the Crown Post and joining and supporting each of the collar beams along the length of the barn.

Ridge Beam

A horizontal timber at the top of the roof (arris) running the length of the barn and securing the tops of all the rafters.

Tie-beam

Substantial transverse timber that sits horizontally between and securing a pair of principal posts and a pair of principal rafters at the arcade or wall plate. The tie beam is jointed by mortice and tenon to the principal posts and acts to restrain the outward thrust generated by the weight of the roof thereby containing the tendency of the principal rafters to spread. The principal rafters are framed into the ends of the tie-beam which is therefore under tension. In cruck frame the tie beam is lapped across each of the blades.

Wind Brace

A bracing timber acting under compression which strengthens the roof structure by stiffening principal rafters and purlins to each of which it is jointed .

Passing Brace

A bracing timber rising diagonally from the groundsill across the wall tie and principal arcade post, to each of which it is trenched or half-lapped, up to the tie-beam..

Scissor Brace

Similar to the passing brace but longer, it continues to rise across the tie-beam to the upper part of the principal rafter on the opposite side of the roof. A second and similar diagonal brace rising from the other side of the barn crossing this brace creates a saltire or scissor effect. These bracing timbers are lapped or trenched to each of the timbers which they pass.

Oak Dowels

Long oak pegs normally tapered to one end. They are hammered through pre-drilled holes to secure two timbers. e.g. through the side of a beam piercing a tenon to prevent its withdrawal from a mortice.

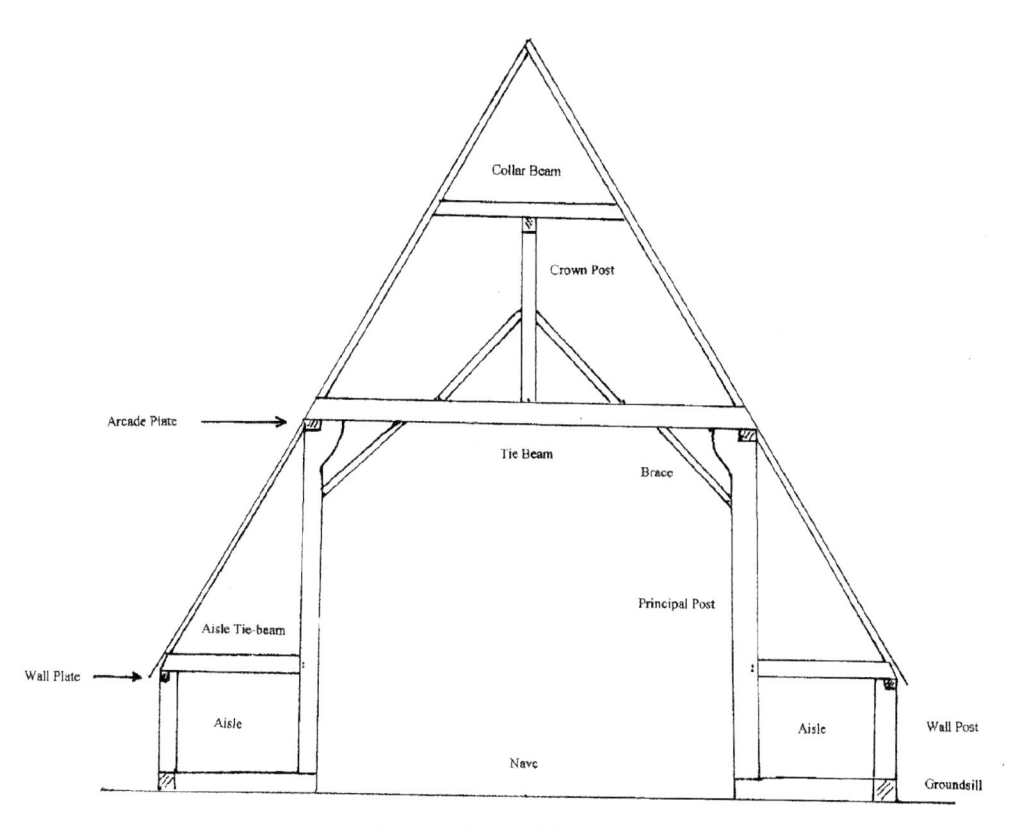

Post and Truss Aisled Barn

1 (ii) Rural Life In The Later Middle Ages - A View

When considering the nature of the great medieval barns in particular the grandness and robustness of their cavernous structural form and the fact they have survived so long we need also to consider their role and importance in rural life and the place of such buildings within the essentially feudal agricultural economy of the period. The term "medieval" refers to the Middle Ages being broadly taken to cover a period of some one thousand years from 500 A.D. to 1500 A.D. in effect post Roman to pre-Tudor (dissolution). In this particular appreciation we are concerned with only the later period from the 11th to the 15th centuries. An annotated schedule of some of the finest early English barns constructed during this period follows later. Photographic illustrations of some of the barns follow that schedule.

Agricultural activity post the Norman Conquest was essentially based upon self-sufficiency with the population of England being some five million in 1345 making its living predominantly by farming the arable land and grazing livestock on the commons, uplands and wastelands. The king, nobility, church and monasteries were the main landowners and the peasantry did the work.

On the broader front England post Conquest (1066) was a land in turmoil as William I sought to impose his authority. Land and buildings were confiscated to reward those that had supported him and to provide for his widespread military defences. He instigated a period of castle building to subjugate the populace and records indicate over one hundred were built by 1100, albeit mostly of

PLATE 4: Bodium Castle, 1386

the motte and bailey form. They served their purpose but timber palisades and towers were susceptible to fire. Later, in the 12th century castles were beginning to be built in stone. The reign of Edward I (1272 -1307), Edward II (1307 - 1327) and Edward III (1327 - 1377) witnessed the building of some of the grandest stone castles many of which still survive to enrich our heritage. Some of the most notable of the whole period include:

- The Keep of the Tower of London (1086 -97) - Kentish ragstone with Caen stone dressings

- The Keep of Colchester Castle in Essex (1090)

- Rochester Castle commenced in 1080 and completed in 1186. The keep is Kentish ragstone with Caen stone dressings

- Caernarfon Castle (1283 - 1323)

- Beaumaris in Anglesey (1295 - 1323)

- Caerphilly, and Conway and Harlech. Bodium Castle in Sussex is dated to 1386 and was built for coastal defence (Plate 4).

The post Conquest era was also a period of church building including great cathedrals e.g. Norwich (1100). Winchester (1079), Worcester (1084), Salisbury (foundation laid in 1220) and monastic buildings, e.g. Rievaulx (1131) and Fountains Abbey (1132). Stone increasingly becomes the material of choice for these great structures. There was clearly much work for the stonemason and his journeymen, quarry workers, labourers and for the master carpenters since much timber was used in the structures and they also provided such as the scaffolding and wooden mouldings for the masons. Records indicate that by the early 13th century Augustinian and Benedictine monastic buildings totalled some 800 compared with 60 in 1086 (Domesday) and by the time of the dissolution there were some 1,000 English monasteries.

The period 1337 - 1453 is termed the One Hundred Years War and was a period of intermittent conflict between England and France. The trigger for the conflicts was Edward III's claim to the French throne in 1337 and subsequently a similar claim by Henry V.

Notable victories against the French were at Crecy (1346) Poitiers (1356) and Agincourt (1415). The armies of the time comprised mostly bands of paid mercenaries. At home, the Wars of the Roses in the mid 15th century (1455 - 1485) were evidence of still further civil unrest.

London's population in the mid 12th century is estimated to have been some 25,000 which increased to about 100,000 (City, Westminster and Southwark) by the mid 1300's. Other comparatively large towns of the period were Norwich with an estimated population of 20,000, York and Bristol about 10,000 each, Winchester some 10,000 - 12,000. For Coventry the estimate is 10,000 and Worcester about 4,000. Whilst in today's terms these densities seem almost irrelevant (there are 15,000 in my local parish of Farnborough in Kent) in the context of the period with typical villages being places averaging about 100/200 people, hamlets even fewer, the "urban" centres had a rapidly growing influence and provided a ready and expanding market for the produce of the land. It is estimated that 10% of the population lived in towns in the 11th century - the rest (90%) were rural dwellers in agriculture or wage labourers. The granting of Royal Charters to hold markets was important for trade and every borough had a market. In addition many markets were also held in villages. There were some 700 towns in England by 1300 and over 1,000 village markets are said to have existed by 1349 and the annual fairs (often lasting up to a week) held around the country added to these centres of trade. It is at this time early forms of credit trading are recorded particularly in the expanding wool and cloth industry. Trade with the continent particularly with the countries of the Rhine Estuaries was long established and with it a form of conduit for the interchange of information

The lords sent their surplus demesne grain to market and wool, hide and animals for sale. The peasants sold some of the produce from their rented land to obtain cash with which to pay their rents, taxes and to buy other goods such as tools, clothing and foodstuffs. The peasants generally lived in spartan single storey dwellings of timber frame (cruck style in Worcester and the Midlands) with wattle and daub walls lime washed and roofs of straw thatch. The bare earth floor would probably have a covering of straw. Within the curtilage of the dwelling it would not be unusual to find a byre or stable for cattle or horse and a barn of modest proportion in which they stored their own produce from their rented arable strips, hay for winter feed for their livestock, and the produce of their garden e.g. vegetables and possibly flax. In the towns evidence of higher grade buildings for merchants and traders is reflected in the presence of some stone built properties but these were not common.

Town Life

Town life in the thirteenth to fifteenth centuries had a structure to it that set the boundaries of everyday activity. Many towns were walled and gated having narrow streets densely lined with tall timber framed buildings, some jettied. The streets were paved with stone and gravel around the gates, market square and Guildhall but elsewhere in the town it might be merely sand and rammed gravel which frequently rutted. Householders were responsible for maintaining the road outside their property and for clearing all their rubbish to areas outside the town walls. The working day except for Sunday was from daybreak to dusk being essentially from the early Mass bell at about 5 a.m. until the curfew bell at 9 p.m. after which any person out walking in the town would be required to carry a lantern and have good cause to be out failing which they could face imprisonment. The beadle, his sergeant and petty constables were responsible for enforcing local regulations, preventing acts of violence and they also served summonses, ensured fire precautions were observed and gave the alarm if fires broke out. They also rostered the watchmen whose duty was to patrol the town after curfew when the town gates would be closed.

The town would daily vibrate with great noise from the clatter of iron rimmed carts and horses' hooves on the gravel and stone paved streets, traders and market stall holders crying their wares, and the smithy hammering and working his metal, and everywhere the bustle of activity as goods were moved and purchases made. The air would be heavy with noxious fumes from the leather tanneries, brew houses, butchers slaughtering beasts, fishmongers' stalls, rotting vegetables on the ground and the filth of open surface drains. Since many householders kept pigs and horses, even cattle, there was an abundance of dung each day to be cleared from stables and pens (probably to cultivated fields outside the town walls). Water was drawn from wells, springs and river and some towns had water piped through lead pipes to the market square. Water carts would convey water for sale. Ale was the normal drink since water was likely to be contaminated by waste and rubbish thrown into the rivers. Foreigners, being broadly anyone not resident in the town, were subject to a toll when they entered the town gates dependent upon the type of cart and its load. The tax raised helped pay for the upkeep of the paved roads particularly around the gate areas and market square. Foreigners were also banned from trading in the market until later in the day to ensure local traders secured the best of the deals. The guilds regulated the trades.

Town life was clearly noisy, arduous and foul smelling with fire an ever present danger and an inadequacy of readily available water when calamities occurred, and there were many.

Village Life

The principal agricultural units however were the village and hamlet within large manorial demesnes, monastic granges and ecclesiastical estates. Large acreages of grain were grown in particular, wheat for milling for bread, rye , barley and oats for inferior bread or for malting and then brewed for ale, peas, beans, hay for forage, flax and hemp, bee keeping for honey and wood coppicing. It is estimated that by 1300 there were some 10,000 wind and water driven mills in England. The peasants, other than freemen, were legally bound to provide labour to the landlord to help farm his demesne lands particularly so at the key periods of ploughing, harrowing, sowing, weeding, harvesting, threshing, etc. and also to undertake the tasks of ditch clearing, hedging, fencing and the repair and maintenance of the local roads and tracks , buildings and barns and seemingly any work their landlord directed. At harvest time the lord generally provided food for the peasants including bread, meat, fish, cheese and ale presumably on the premise of self interest since a frail peasant would not be able to undertake this prolonged and heavy work. The peasants also rented land from the demesne to farm for the provision for their own families. Rents were paid in kind (produce) and/or in cash.

In the less populated West and the North of England farming generally took the form of pastoral grazing whereas in the Midlands and the South of England arable farming predominated and was organised on the two or three Open Field system with fallow rests. These large unfenced fields were subdivided into many narrow strips with the peasants each cultivating a number of widely scattered strips. This ensured they each had a share of the variations in soil types, slopes and valley locations (and therefore micro climate variations). Some of the strips would be in proximity to the village or hamlet, therefore more easily accessed for cultivation and manuring. Other more problematic strips were much further afield. Co-operation between peasants was a prerequisite in determining what was grown on the strips and what was fallow or grazing. Peasants with an inadequacy of land to be self-sufficient could sell their labour and work on the larger farms.

Amongst the lower order the special craft skills of carpentry, blacksmithing, tanner, builder, thatcher, etc. developed regulated by the craft guilds which existed in each of the towns and cities. Transport was difficult, roads were not metalled, often merely tracks, pack horses and ox cart were the main means of carrying loads. Travel was therefore particularly slow, tiring and expensive. River and coastal waters were also of importance.

Slavery, present at the time of the Conquest, was held to have mostly ceased in England by 1200. Whilst the peasants, (serfs) remained subject to the law of the baronial court freemen attained the right of appeal to be heard before the Royal Courts. Magna Carta (1215) set out a charter of liberties restraining the power of the king and Habeas Corpus provided that "due cause" must be shown for a person to be denied his liberty rather than the earlier process of detention "by order". Within the village life for the peasantry was dominated by the more wealthy landholders but the whole remained under the control of the landlord through his bailiffs and reeve.

The vast Church and monastic estates were in many instances divided between retained demesne and fields in strip holdings rented to the peasantry. Some of the larger estates were important for sheep grazing for the growing woollen industry in the 14th century. Trade included the supply of wool to Flemish and Italian merchants. Cloth was also traded, in particular the fine broadcloths from Stamford,

Lincoln, Louth, Beverly and York and later the Cotswolds, Stroudwaters and Castle Combes. The invention of the water powered fulling mill replacing the earlier labour intensive hand and foot methods had the effect of relocating the industry from the towns to the rural areas. Records indicate that by the end of the 13th century 80 fulling mills had been built in England but by the 14th century these fulling mills were widespread and many monastic and ecclesiastical estates had such mills. The number of mills for grinding corn is estimated at 6,000 in 1086, rising to 10,000 by 1300.

Ploughing on the arable lands had to be undertaken on a co-operative basis since few peasants had a plough or oxen, being teams of six or eight to achieve the task. Progress was very slow ploughing about half of one acre a day and it took therefore considerable time and labour to cultivate the large open fields. With the gradual replacement of the ox by the horse productivity and acreage ploughed per day rapidly increased (about 1 acre per day). Crop yields were significantly lower than in modern times. In broad measure it is assessed as a six fold increase in weight in modern times compared with medieval yields. (Volume and weight of the grain have both increased). Harvesting was by hand using the scythe and sickle, stacking the sheaves of corn into stooks (comprising six to eight bundles) in the fields to aid drying, hand loading by pitchfork to the haywagon, conveyance of the corn to the barn by wagon or ox cart for storage and later hand threshing the corn with the flail in winter winnowing the chaff from the grain and storage of the grain in the granary, a lengthy relentlessly hard and dirty labour. The number of cart journeys required to convey corn from the fields to the barn would have been considerable and some records indicate in excess of a hundred such laborious journeys were required to move a single crop.

Meadowland and common land were vital for the provision of hay crops for winter fodder the absence of which otherwise necessitated the early slaughter of livestock and hindered the development of larger herds. Rough wasteland was gradually being improved to increase the area of pasture for sheep grazing and for arable (assarting) cultivation, pigs fattened on acorns in the woodlands (pannage). Land drainage and marshland reclamation works were undertaken by the great Abbeys, in particular the fens of Eastern England, the Somerset levels, Holderness in Yorkshire and the North East Kent coastal area and at Pevensey.

A major change in agricultural life resulted from the severe harvest failures in 1315 - 1316 and 1321 and the sheep diseases in 1313 - 1317 and cattle diseases in 1319 - 1321 and subsequently the Black Death in 1348/9 and its recurrence in 1361, 1368 - 69. England's population is held to have fallen from some 5 million to 2.5 million in the late 14th century with the consequence that labour became a scarce resource. The impact of the Black Death in restricting labour availability and creating a surplus of unused land had the crucial effect of diluting the practice of forced labour on the lords' demesne (there were not enough peasants to do the work) and it was increasingly the practice to rent out more of the demesne to the peasants with the lord content to receive a guaranteed income in cash (and or produce) as opposed to being dependent upon a price fluctuating market for the sale of surplus grain and other crops. Land enclosures also increased as arable was replaced by the more profitable sheep and cattle grazing. Over 2,000 villages and hamlets were deserted the occupants having died or migrated.

Craftsmen migrated to where their skills were required, carpenters, thatchers, woodcutters, turners, charcoal burners, lime burners, smiths, salt boilers, ironworkers, leatherworkers, quarrymen, etc. Labourers moved to where work opportunities were more favourable particularly to the growing urban areas.

In 1381 the counties of Kent, Essex and East Anglia witnessed an uprising of the peasantry. The grinding harshness of life for the lower order compared with the quality of life enjoyed by nobility had resulted in long-term and widespread simmering discontent. This discontent over spilled to rebellion when a new poll tax was imposed in 1380. Mass evasion of the tax occurred (reminiscent perhaps of the disquiet and considerable evasion of the 20th century poll tax). Attempts at enforcement erupted into violence. In June, 1381, it is recorded there was a march of some 5,000 - 10,000 to London with consequent pillage and burning of property and records. The peasants demanded an end to their serfdom and, among other things, wanted a new Magna Carta. Concessions were granted by the king and the disturbances abated. Local sheriffs were then ordered to restore peace at any cost. One can imagine the many hangings and imprisonments that followed. The rebellion was quelled but life for the lower order of peasants remained grim.

PLATE 6: **Carmelite Priory**
Buildings with 13th century Pilgrims' Hall on extreme right

By 1500 most English peasants rented their land on the basis of a cash payment and or in produce. The need to provide labour to the lord to work his demesne rapidly declined. Labour was now very scarce and came at a price.

We see the rise of the Copyholder whereby the peasantry pay rent fixed in amount of money or produce (not labour) The terms were entered in the court records of the manor following which a copy of the entry was given to the tenant or the "copyholder". If the terms were complied with the land tenancy remained secure and subject to the payment of a fee could be passed down to the copyholder's heirs.

Shortly after the end of the 16th century despite the ravages of the Black Death the population had slowly recovered and grown to some five million. Up until the dissolution of the monasteries when some 800 properties and lands were destroyed or seized in the 1530 - 1540s (during the reign of Henry VIII) they had played an important, even dominant, role in the period (Plates 5 and 6 illustrate the 13th century

PLATE 5: **Carmelite Priory Gatehouse**
Aylesford (15th century)

Carmelite Priory at Aylesford and the 15th century gatehouse). The abbeys and priories owned large tracts of land some of which were retained to provide produce to feed their religious community including the lay brothers and hence the need for large barns in which to store the produce until required. Other land was rented out and the cash rents used to purchase other goods required by the monastery. Fish ponds were common for supplementing diets. The term grange was used to indicate a monastic farm and a number of large barns associated with these farms still survive e.g. as at Coggeshall in Essex which has recently been restored. Some of the stone barns are of substantial structure and architecturally elaborate such as the Great Barn at Abbotsbury Abbey in Dorset Torre Abbey Barn in Devon and Buckland Abbey Barn . E. King (Modern England from Hastings to Bosworth) refers to an interesting quotation dated July, 1108. "Hugh of Ropsley in Lincolnshire was sent a writ of Henry I issued at Brompton, outside of Huntingdon, ordering him to allow the monks of Belvoir in Leicestershire to collect their tithes at the door of his barn in peace. If you do not do this the Bishop of Lincoln and Ralph Basset will see to it". Relations between landowners and monasteries were clearly not always harmonious.

The tithe barn was normally of more modest proportions and located in proximity to the church their function being to store the tithe produce (wheat, barley, oats, rye, root crops, beans, etc. and all manner of other produce) collected from the parishioners being for the support of the parish church and the relief of the poor. The tithe was in effect a tax of one tenth part of the crop but records indicate it also included a wide range of produce, e.g. items such as hop poles and bundles of faggots, wool fleeces and hides. Barn storage was essential to secure and keep dry the produce until needed. The Revd. E. L. Cutts (Parish Priests and Their People in the Middle Ages in England) comments upon the simple nature of the clergy house in the sixteenth and seventeenth centuries with land holdings including stables, hay houses and barns, e.g. 1534 - Allington Rectory, Kent : house with mill house, boulting house, gatehouse plus barn next to the gate and a second barn near the church.

1610 -   Ingatestone Rectory : house with dove house, stable and barn in very ruinous condition ,

1610 -   Ingrove Rectory : house, milk house, poultry house, hay house, stable and barn.

1610 -   Little Bromley Rectory, Essex : large parsonage house with mote and gate house, stable, hay house, and a barn measuring 75ft. long and 27ft. wide with 79. 5 acres of glebe land.

1341 Durham: Among the many works undertaken during the time of John Fossor prior of Durham (1341 - 1374) in addition to many works on church buildings were many involving farm buildings e.g. construction of a great barn for the hay of the guesthouse, a great stable and forge, a new roof over the brewhouse and the bakehouse, a malthouse and a great granary, a barn at Estrington and another barn at Allerton. A further barn at West Flodgat and at Pittington and a mill and bakehouse. A great barn in the manor of Rainton plus a mill, a new barn in the manor of Dalton and in the manor of Heyworth, a barn and a water mill. A tithe barn at Harton and a new windmill at Southwike and another at Hesilden. A great barn in the manor of "Belu" and a mill at "Oventon Belu" and a granary. A granary at Belassis, a water mill at Billingham and mills at Wolston and Bernpton and a water mill at Ketton. A mill at Merington and a barn , a byre and a kiln. A mill at Fery and at Aclif and a new barn at Hoghall. (Extract from L. S. Salzman p. 392/393).

This detailed record indicates a period of considerable building activity and substantial expense the works being undertaken during the prior's period of tenure of some thirty years and at a time when the plague was ravaging the country. The prevalence of barns, granaries and mills would indicate a considerable acreage of grain crops as do the malt house and brew house.

The Commutation of Tithes Act of 1836 brought to an end the legal requirement to pay a tenth of the parish produce to the church but well prior to this (early Anglo-Saxon practice) it had substantially declined to be replaced by money payment. It is interesting to note that for Coggeshall in Essex commutation is claimed not to have come into effect until 1851 (despite the law to the contrary) one doubts whether this was the only exception.

In summary the role of the great barns of the period can be seen as providing essential dry storage and security for all the agricultural produce, be it the tithe produce for the church, the monastic grange produce for the religious community, or produce for the landlord's household from his demesne lands. Other large barns were located at a distance in the outlying fields for more convenient access and storage of grain and crops. Each of these barns provided the focus for much rural activity and hard work with the heavy work in the fields followed by laborious cartage of bulky, heavy produce and corn from the fields by ox cart or horse wagon to the barns, stacking and storing the crops in the barn, transport of the surplus crops from the barn from time to time to markets for sale, and in the winter the labour intensive threshing of the corn and shelter and feeding for animals. The barns were a vital part of the local community and a clear focus for much of the local activity. With improved agricultural practices and land reclamation resulting in much more land coming into arable cultivation and increases in crop yields the large barns remained essential throughout the period.

However, as trading developed boosted by the rapid growth of the towns and cities so agriculture became more mixed farming with enclosure of fields for sheep and cattle for the supply of meat to satisfy the increasing urban demand together with the growth of the wool trade for export it was inevitable their role would diminish. Eventually it was as a consequence of the mechanisation of agriculture particularly in the 18th and 19th centuries with the introduction of machine drills, improved plough, horse drawn reapers and threshing machine and later in the 20th century the more common use of tractors and the combine harvester that the need for these traditional barns went into steep decline. They had served their time and now faced neglect, demolition or conversion. Many of the great barns have been lost but the endeavour of both the National Trust, English Heritage and the many local preservation trusts have secured some of the finest barns for posterity and many have a positive practical community use as "event" centres and for local activities. As part of our cultural history it is important the barns are retained and nurtured.

1(iii) Population Trends :
11ᵗʰ - 16ᵗʰ Century

To assist in fully appreciating the importance of the barn in the later medieval period the earlier paragraphs provide a short summary illuminating the nature of rural life in England demonstrating the dominant role of agriculture particularly the widespread practice of a subsistence form of land cultivation.   The village represented the main centre for everyday life with the many barns being focal points around which considerable activity and much hard and dirty labouring revolved. Domesday Book (1086) indicates some 100 towns existed each having a population of about 2000 people but only 10% of the population lived in towns at the end of the 11ᵗʰ century. This proportion increased to 20% by 1300 as the urban areas expanded but remained constant at this level to the 1520's. Life expectancy would be thirty to forty years with infant and child mortality rates very high.

The reader's perception of this, to modern eyes, harsh and primitive style of feudal life endured by the many will be enhanced by a consideration of the broad trends in population throughout the period. The following figures provide clarity in the sense of scale, indicate the significant changes in availability or otherwise of labour and factors affecting labour mobility leading to the growing importance of the towns, expansion of trade and industry and eventually in the 19th and 20th century the consequential rapid decline in the relevance and usefulness of the large traditional barns.

The population baseline derives from the Domesday Book which, subject to certain qualifications, provided an arithmetic calculation of the population of England in 1086. The detailed survey of the shires, counties, hundreds, boroughs and villages provide the starting point against which to measure trends over the next four centuries and resulted from surveys undertaken by special commissioners sent by the king (William I) to assess the wealth in terms of landholdings, livestock, buildings and population of the country and particularly who held that wealth. Evidence was taken on oath from the most significant people in each area surveyed , in particular the sheriff, barons, priests, reeves, and representatives of the villagers. The area surveys were first recorded in subordinate books, e.g. the Domesday Monochorum of Christchurch, Canterbury, Exeter Domesday and Regional returns from e.g. Ely Abbey. The mass of the survey documentation was then collated at Winchester. The whole study is claimed to have been completed in less than twelve months but the areas of Durham, Northumberland, Westmoreland and Cumberland were omitted as were some towns. The population figures for 1086 are summarised below. However the survey recorded only the heads of each household therefore considerable debate has ensued over many years among the historians as to how these base figures can be realistically translated into full population numbers. After allowing for estimated birth rates, infant mortality rates (assessed to be high) adult mortality and including allowance for famine, pestilence and wars (the Malthus factor) the consensus appears to have focused upon a multiplier of x 5. Provision had also to be made for the population of the missing counties and for some omitted towns. The result was a total estimated population at 1086 of some 1.6 million of which 150,000 were slaves. More recent estimates have put forward the view that the population was nearer to 2 - 2.5 million.

We should not consider the matter of population without some reference to the work of T. R. Malthus who published his first "Essay on the Principles of Population" in 1798, his central argument being any increase in population is limited by the means of subsistence therefore it follows as the means of subsistence expands so will population. The major restraints upon such increases are the consequences of war, pestilence and famine. If we consider records contained in the Anglo-Saxon Chronicle for the period post Roman to the twelfth century we see a clear reflection of the Malthus thesis. This lengthy time appears to be one long brutal and bloody history of internal conflict and murderous dark deeds exacerbated by warring foreign incursions with considerable and regular destruction to property and life. Throughout the whole of this period is woven a recurrence of severe famine and pestilence including severe murrain of cattle. It seems therefore as subsistence may be capable of expansion by bringing more land into cultivation or its more intensive cultivation in an era when manual labour and the ox were the primary power sources the absence of productive manpower will itself provide an effective break upon population growth that can only be remedied over time.

Slaves - Domesday Book

(from Domesday Book/Kent by P. Morgan)

A sample taken from Domesday records for Kent indicate that in addition to land areas, plough teams, mills, population, etc, the following slaves were identified.

Faversham	5	30 villagers, 40 smallholders and a mill, 5 slaves
Larkfield	8	40 villagers, 5 smallholders and a mill, 8 slaves - Land of King William I
Dartford	3	142 villagers, 10 smallholders, a mill and two harbours, 3 slaves
Darenth	6	22 villagers, 7 cottagers and 2 mills, 6 slaves
Otford	8	101 villagers, 18 smallholders and 6 mills, 8 slaves
Sundridge	8	27 villagers, 9 smallholders and a church, 8 slaves. Land of the Archbishop of Canterbury
Wrotham	10	76 villagers, 18 smallholders and 3 mills, 10 slaves

Southfleet	7	25 villagers, 9 smallholders and a church, 7 slaves
Stone	4	20 villagers, 12 smallholders and a church and mill, 4 slaves
Fawkham	3	15 villagers, 3 smallholders and 2 mills, 3 slaves. Land of the Bishop of Rochester
Snodland	5	10 villagers, 6 smallholders and a church and 3 mills, 5 slaves
Frindsbury	9	40 villagers, 28 smallholders and church and a mill, 9 slaves

There are numerous further such references to slaves. Slaves could be bought and sold. However by the early 13th century they had merged with the general peasantry and slavery had virtually ceased to exist - rural poverty remained.

England : Domesday Population 1086

(estimate adapted from H. Darby, Domesday England)

Category	Population	Description
Burgesses	120,000	Urban dwellers in the main towns, including bakers, tailors, shoemakers, cooks, porters
Freemen	190,000	
Villeins	572,000	Villagers who rent land and provide labour services to the landlord. Rent paid in produce and /or cash.

Category	Population	Description
Bordars) Cottars)	460,000	Bordars were smallholders having generally less land than villeins. Cottars had gardens but normally little or no land. Both owed labour services to the landlord
Slaves	150,000	Provide labour on the manorial lands where they were given shelter and fed. Slaves could be and were sold.
Others	103,000	Nobility, priests, plus estimated population for the northern counties.
TOTAL	1,595,000	

Some 10% of the population lived in the towns with 90% in the rural areas. Great care is required when interpreting the figures. Significant estimating was involved by those who created these base line totals and some historians have chosen to take a rounded total of 2 million for the 11th century base figure from which to monitor subsequent trends.

Just prior to the Black Death in the mid 14th century the estimated population had grown to some 5 million (dependant upon which source reference is used). The early 14th century was a period of agrarian crisis with harvest failures in 1315, 1316 and 1321. At the same time severe diseases in sheep in 1313 - 1317 and cattle in 1319 - 21 resulted in increased hardship for the peasantry. Many died and incomes were depressed. The devastating plagues of 1348/49 and later, 1361 and 1368/69 virtually halved the population down to some 2.5 million This severe reversal had major consequences for rural life in the sense that labour became a very scarce and expensive commodity with most villages heavily depopulated some 2000 even abandoned with arable land left uncultivated.

The monastic orders had by the mid 1300's some 1,000 religious houses of greater or lesser size in England and totalled some 17,000 monks, friars, nuns and lay brothers. They too were severely affected by the plagues but by the early 16th century it is estimated their numbers were 10,000 monks and 2,000 nuns. By the mid 16th century the general population had recovered to some 3 million and by this time slavery had long disappeared and the former requirement of labour services from the villagers had been replaced by payment in cash or produce. By the early 17th century the population had again reached 5 million.

British Historical Statistics (B. R. Mitchell)
Pre-Censal Estimates of Population for England

1541	2,774,000	
1551	3,011,000	
1600	4,066,000	
1635	5,035,000	
1700	5,027,000	
1750	5,739,000	
1794	8,101,000	
1801	8,893,000	(Males - 4,255,000, Females - 4,638,000) (England and Wales)
1811	10,164,000	
1821	12,000,000	(Males - 5,850,000 Females - 6,150,000) (England and Wales)

The first census of population was in 1801 and again in 1811, 1821 and 1831 but the detailed records were not preserved. The census on the 7th June, 1841, represents the first detailed records. Census of population were carried out at 10 yearly intervals thereafter. Civil registration of births is held to have become effective about 1841 although this latter point is not universally accepted and perhaps a 5% under recording factor argued by some historians seems appropriate.

Population Trends of Some Principal Towns

By 1300 it is estimated there were 700 towns in England but some had as little as 300 inhabitants and many towns were unwalled and lacked charter status. 50 towns had more than 2000 people but the majority were about 600. Great care is essential interpreting these figures due to many estimating factors and inevitable boundary changes over the lengthy period of time.

Estimated Population

Town	1150	1348/1500	1800
London	25,000	100,000 (including the City, Westminster and Southwark)	959,000 (for the county)
York		10,000	17,000
Norwich		20,000	36,000
Bristol		10,000	61,000
Winchester		12,000	
Coventry		10,000	16,000
Worcester		4,000	11,000
Birmingham		2,000	71,000
Canterbury		5,000	
Lincoln		5,000	
Gloucester		5,000	
Oxford		5,000	
Exeter		4,000	

The major ports in the 13th and 14th centuries in addition to London included Southampton, Sandwich, Kings Lynn, Boston, Hull and Newcastle each having populations of some 5,000.

The impact of the Great Plague in the mid 14th century would have decimated the figures for that period. Recovery is achieved by the end of the 16th century including migration factors and the trend figures have credibility. In 1688 a labour force analysis indicated that of 1.4 million families, 16.4% of the total families in England and Wales were still involved in agriculture and in addition Cottagers and Paupers are recorded at 22.5%.

By 1801 agricultural families total 14.6% plus agricultural labourers 15.5% and cottagers and paupers 11.9%. Sadly, it is noted that vagrant families are recorded at 8.2% substantially up on the 1688 figures (1.7%) but probably more accurately compiled than the earlier assessment. The 1801 analysis demonstrates the increasing importance of industry and commerce at 24.7% and 9.4% of families respectively, with military and maritime categories recorded at 11.1%. The growth in urban settlements reflected in the sample figures above further emphasises the emergence of a large market for agricultural produce and the growing importance of trade and industry.

1 (iv) Medieval Building: Organisation and Techniques

England is fortunate to be blessed with a rich cultural heritage manifest in the built environment by the great palaces, castles, monasteries, cathedrals, parish churches, stately homes and associated great estates which together embrace the surviving tithe barns and monastic grange barns with which this book is principally concerned. These many buildings, most of which can trace their origins to the medieval period, albeit with later modifications, new additions or major renovations illustrate the sophisticated building skills of the mason with intricate, ornate carving yet being massive stone structures notably fine in jointing and decorative in detail; and complex framed timber structures with a wealth of jointing forms that glorify the craft skill of the master carpenter.

   The perception is of an early development of craftsmanship and with it extensive practical knowledge of advanced engineering and design and construction skills, a concept that sits uncomfortably with a generally held understanding that the late middle ages was a period of little general education for other than the ecclesiastics, monks and nobility, the country predominantly a feudal economy with the great majority of the population of peasant status owing labour services to the lords and renting small land holdings from which to scrape a form of subsistence living. Clearly, this latter general interpretation cannot sensibly reflect the true nature of the period and more recent historical studies have advanced strong well supported arguments to challenge this perception. The conclusion has to be that the period showed great diversity with the influence of the growing urban centres bringing with it well developed trade guilds that rigorously controlled their specific specialisms both through control over admission to the trade, provision of education and training particularly through a system of apprenticeships, regulation of the trade including standards and protection by ensuring outsiders did not intrude on their trade activity within the particular town. The trade guilds were many, over one hundred are identified in the late 14th century to include, weavers, drapers, spicers, tanners, maltsters, arrowsmiths, etc. and the general merchant classes.

It is to the freemen particularly that we must look to identify the source of manpower that underwent education and training within the great craft guilds, particularly those of the masons and the carpenters. It was they who generally were free to travel around the country and practice their skills wherever the demand existed. It was normal for craft apprenticeships to be for a period of seven years commencing from around 14 - 15 years and concluding at the age of 21 - 22 years following which they became journeymen to continue their learning until achieving master craftsmen status. The craft guilds regulated their members, controlled admissions - normally only sons of freemen, arranged education and training for the apprentices, set standards for the craft even, it appears, controlling template designs for specific aspects of ornate building styles.

The view has been advanced that the peasant class owing labour services to their lord and needing to spend long periods of time cultivating their strips of land would have inadequate spare time to pursue the lengthy training necessary to join the craft guilds. The guilds' tight control over entry conditions and fees would also present a formidable constraint. Following from the above we need to consider how the great buildings were planned, designed and built. We know the skilled labour came from the craft guilds but how was a particular project organised and what building facilities were available. We need to again consider the role of the craft guilds which trace their existence well back into the medieval period. Such guilds existed for a wide range of building skills of which the masons must feature as the principal guild particularly for building in stone and arguably representing the precursors to the later title of Architect with the connotations of design as well as technical ability that title encompasses.

The master carpenter of the guild of carpenters was the principal for building with timber, framing, and for roofing the great stone structures and also for providing much of the formwork, scaffolding and cutting wooden templates to the mason's design. Many of the other crafts were regulated by guild companies including smiths, glaziers, plumbers, joiners and tilers, etc. At an early stage it appears a single master craftsman, be it mason or carpenter, would have overall responsibility for a major building project. It would be part of their responsibility to bring together sufficient skilled labour and general labourers to undertake the various building tasks be it preparing foundations, carting materials, rough masons to hew broken stone into coarse cubical blocks, stonecutters who worked the blocks into fine shaped blocks of ashlar ready for laying, and other masons who would specialise in carving circular stonework to be used for voussoirs (concave curves) of arches or convex shapes for the building of drums (slices) for construction of circular piers.

The master freemason, being competent in each of these skills would oversee, direct and control the daily work schedules and make provision for the raw material supplies of stone, mortar material and equipment some of which may be provided by the client be it the king, nobles, monastery, church or lord of the manor. He would also be responsible for co-ordination of the other crafts and have overall direct responsibility to whoever had commissioned the project for the designated site.

Where the master carpenter was the principal for a timber project be it a tithe barn, framing for a manor house or the roofing of a church, it would be normal for him to arrange for the necessary timbers and skilled labour, for felling designated trees to provide the substantial jowled posts, pit and trestle sawing for planks, rafters and studding, craft labour for cutting the mortices, tenons and other joints for framing, shaping the great roof trusses, and preparing timber for bracing the roofing members and for tie beams, collars and purlins that effectively lock the frame and the roof together. As with the master mason, the master carpenter would have responsibility to contract with the blacksmith to provide all metalwork, iron straps, hinges and bolts and all manner of nails for the fixings. The smith would also make, repair and sharpen the tools and equipment used by the other craftsmen and consequently would have a close working and continuous relationship with most building construction projects. Quite separate from these "mobile" freemen of the craft guilds were those who were directly associated with the royal palaces and ecclesiastical houses. This latter would include the cathedral, masons and carpenters workshops and also some of the lay brothers of the monasteries. It is argued the latter may have originally trained with the guilds and later in life converted to the church.

Having briefly addressed the nature of building organisation and the dominant role of master mason or master carpenter as the focal point to direct major projects we then need to consider the building techniques in common use during the later middle ages. A recently published book by Gunther Binding presents the results of many years research travelling principally across Europe and displays some six hundred illustrations being drawings highlighting representations portrayed in hundreds of medieval illuminated Bibles, psalters and manuscripts, other early printed works, stained glass windows, wood panels, paintings, sculptures and architectural stone and wood carvings, embroidery, wall and floor mosaics, tapestries and enamels each depicting building work with craftsmen at their tasks tackling stone and timber at various stages of preparation and construction and authenticated to special time periods ranging from the 12th to the 15th centuries.

It is quite clear from these representations of craft workmanship the range of hand tools and equipment available through the later middle ages was considerable and the equipment for moving and lifting heavy stonework whilst dependent upon "muscle" did include simple pulley and rope with spoked capstan and treadmill power. However, preparation of materials had to be done by hand. A summary of a sample of equipment and tools and uses is set out below.

We rightly marvel at the immensity of what the early craftsmen achieved knowing the range of tools at their disposal. Craftsmen of today with their powered tools, sawmills for stone and timber cutting, steel scaffolding, diesel powered loaders, JCBs, powered cranes, etc., would be hard pressed to achieve the quality of these early structures that have successfully survived the ravages of time. Health and Safety regulate today's building sites but in these earlier times such practices did not exist and safety methods were discovered by trial and error and the process of elimination as buildings collapsed or supports failed and grave personal injuries and general calamities resulted. It was a hard school in which to learn and some of the illustrations depict workmen falling from high towers.

The pictorial evidence referred to above being so widespread in source materials and location and authenticated in date provides a realistic and acceptable basis for support of the type of tools available to the medieval craftsmen and of their methods of working. Other supportive evidence would be inventory lists of tools recorded at various locations and in wills. These indicate interalia the variety of saws used including large two handed saws for pit sawing, hammers and chisels including bolsters, wood planes, axes of various types for stone or wood, mallets, augers and braces, etc. The instruments of the Master Mason were the compass, set square, straight edge and plumb line and indicate a sound knowledge of building geometry. A variety of template/mouldings would also be normal to guide the stone cutters in shaping their ashlar blocks.

Hammers with two pointed iron heads were used to shape rough stone slabs. Other hammers with serrated edges were used for coarse stone work and axes tended to be used for final smoothing. Chisels and bolster chisels were available for carving and fine work. Mallet and lump hammer were also used. The carpenter used a variety of saws including a two handed saw for cutting large timbers., two man frame saws used for cutting beams or planks, short saws with thinner blades for general cutting. The auger and brace would be used to drill holes in timber for dowel fixings, and to start the cutting of mortices, the adze and chisel would be used to complete the joint. Axes of various types were used for felling trees and for shaping and working large beams. Even wood planes similar to block planes seen today were available for finishing work on the smaller scantlings. The timber, normally oak, was used unseasoned since it was easier to work in that condition and additionally gave an immediacy to its use. The alternative would be lengthy delay with much capital tied up as the green timber was allowed to dry.

Lifting mechanisms included simple pulley and rope aided by

spoked capstans for greater turning power. The use of treadmill for powering the simple crane structure is also illustrated. Blocks of stone would be gripped by the lewis mechanism for lifting to higher levels. Ladders of conventional design were common, other forms included long planks with wooden bars fixed at rung intervals across the plank. Carriage of heavy stone weights to the site included the use of four or two wheeled ox drawn carts. Handcarts and wheelbarrows aided movement about the site and panniers - a carrying device similar to a stretcher and carried by two men were also common. Crowbars were used to ease blocks into position. Scaffolding was of timber and took various forms including long poles erected vertically with horizontal poles lashed at the crossings. Connection of the scaffold to the wall structure was by other timbers inserted into the walls and cemented in. The working platform on these structures would be planks or wicker hurdles lashed into position.

Another type of scaffold regularly illustrated shows thick timbers set into wall slots left as construction progressed, protruding to the inside of the wall. These projecting timbers are then supported by struts that run diagonally from the wall beneath i.e. there is no vertical support from ground level. Overlaying these projecting timbers would be planking or wicker hurdles.

Building foundations : records indicate that where ground was poor and needed stabilising to carry great weight wood piling may be used, great timbers being driven by rams into the ground. In other cases a depth of rubble would be spread. Some foundations would be trenched to solid rock levels.

The organisation and equipment available to the medieval craftsmen seem not unfamiliar to us today except for the absence of electric or motorised power facility and nowadays the greater division of responsibility between crafts and the normally separate role for architect and project manager. Medieval work would of course be slower but quality appears unsurpassed.

Having demonstrated the general organisation, approach and techniques of medieval building we now focus again on the great barn structures and the following examples help bring some reality to construction issues. In 1434 a barn was built at Ormesby in Norfolk for which timber costing £1. 2s. 10d. was purchased and carried from

Norwich at a cost of eight shillings and eight pence. The carpenter, William Berry, then framed the barn for a lump sum of £3. 13s. 4d. While a stonemason with his servant built the footing getting six shillings and 3d. for seven and one half days work by the two men. At the raising of the barn one shilling and two pence was spent on bread, ale and cheese to celebrate. The framed buildings were normally raised upon low walls prepared to receive them and a crane or sheerlegs with cable and tackle was necessary to pull the frame into the vertical position. The frame was then propped up by raking shores fitted into oblique slots cut near the top of the main posts to stabilise it while further framing continued. The grange barn at Winscombe in Somerset was retiled in 1393-94 with 6,000 stone tiles from Ifracombe bought at Radcliff (Bristol) at three shillings and four pence per thousand.

Travelling expenses were paid to craftsmen for journeys on official business including the expense of carrying the craftsmen's tools. In 1418 the Chapter of Wells had to pay the expenses of their master carpenter to travel from Wells to Burnham to supervise the building of a barn. This included one shilling and one pence for the hire of a horse to carry the carpenter's tools to Burnham and back including feedstuffs for the horse.

In 1426-27 when building the barn at Harmondsworth in Middlesex the following nails were purchased from the blacksmith John Deresford :

- 250   Spykenayll

- 350   fyfstroknayll

- 2   Goosefeet

- 2   Woodcock bills

- 12   Gumphs (hooks or gudgeon pins)

The cost of these iron nails and iron fixings was 2d. per lb. weight for 200lbs. of iron. Carriage costs were four shillings. (Each of these four illustrations are taken from J. Harvey, Medieval Craftsmen).

Salzman records in his "Buildings in England Down to 1540" that in 1376 a great barn had been bought at Wimbledon for £8, dismantled and removed to Shene where it was re-erected to be used for storing the king's hay there.

1472   at Farnham rectory, fourteen shillings were paid for oak posts, braces, baulks (tie-beams) as one parcel to construct a barn. Three shillings and nine pence were paid for fifteen pairs of rafters for the roof being three pence per couple.

1454 -   five score sheaves of reeds called thackrede were supplied for the "watlyng" under the plaster of a barn at Uffington.

1470 -   at Penshurst, reference is made to "radelyng" (plaster with clay) and daubing of the walls of the barn and the carriage of clay, called "lombe" for the said work.

         In Caldicote in Hertfordshire a tenant built two very large barns capable of holding all the crops grown on his 160 acres of arable land (quote from C. Dyer "Everyday Life in Medieval England").

1478   Exeter : Malthouse. An agreement made in April by a mason to build a malthouse twenty foot long and fourteen foot wide comprising two storeys, the base to be of lime and stone sleeper walls two feet high to support three timber crucks for the roof and with mud infilled walls ten foot high. A middle floor to be set upon two timber cross beams with a stairway, doors and windows. Also, to construct a drain to carry away the water from the brew house into the street. The work to be completed by Michaelmas. For this the mason shall be paid £8 in three instalments and the mason is to give a bond of £10 for the performance of his contract (Salzman - page 540).

         Remuneration of labour during the period reviewed above was governed by the Statute of Labourers 1349 and 1351which sought to control wage levels after the onset of the Black Death which had devastated the available labour force.

- Master Carpenter   3d. per day
- Freemason   4d. per day
- Other masons   3d. per day
- Tilers   3d. per day
- Assistants   1 1/2d. per day

These rates compare with the London Regulation of Building Trades Wages of 1212 e.g. Freemasons and carpenters - 3d. per day plus food or 4d. without and masons and tilers 1 1/2d. per day plus food or 3d. without. By 1446 a freemason or master carpenters' wage was 4d. with food or 5 1/2d. without. Lower wages were paid in the winter months due to shorter working hours and the working day was from dawn until dusk but with breaks for breakfast and dinner.

The above figures help to put building construction costs in context for the relevant period bearing in mind there were 240 pence in the pound and twenty shillings in the pound.

The Early English Barn

I(v). Annotated Schedule of Some Early English Barns

I(vi). Schedule of Illustrated Barns

A Representative Selection of Early English Barns

County Location	Date Built	Construction	Comment
Cumbria			
Augustinian Priory of St. Mary's Carlisle Tithe Barn	c. 1490	Eight bays on east/west axis 115ft. long x 27ft wide. Walls were red sandstone 3ft. 7ins. thick. North side was open with vertical posts 20ins. x 15ins. thick supporting the roof trusses Tie beams measured 30ft. x 21ins.	Restoration commenced in 1969 and the barn is now used as a parish hall and for community activities
Devon			
Torre Abbey Barn, Torquay	c. 1300	Stone walls, tile roof, porch sited midway between the ten buttresses.	Torre Abbey founded in 1196
Buckland Abbey Barn	c.1300	Stone walls, slate roof. buttressed, one large porch 159ft. x 32ft x 40ft high.	Arch braced roof Tithe barn Cistercian Abbey
Dorset			
Abbotsbury Abbey Abbey Barn	c.1400	Stone walls, buttressed, thatch roof, gable, no aisles, two porches, 31ft.wide	276 feet long
East Sussex			
Alciston	c. 1400	Post and truss, aisled barn of L shape, flint walls, tile roof. 170ft. Long.	Battle Abbey lands
Court Farm, Falmer	c. 1400	Post and truss, half hipped thatch roof, weather boarded, flint walls.	
Exceat, Cuckmere Valley	c. 1750	Timber framed, post and truss, flint walls, tile roof.	East Sussex County Council Barn now used as a visitor centre

County Location	Date Built	Construction	Comment
East Sussex			
Great Dixter	c. 1750	Post and truss, clay tile roof. King Post, weather boarded.	Oasthouse built 1890
Essex			
Coggeshall Grange Barn (originally part of a Cistercian Monastery Grange)	1250	Timber frame, post and truss, six bays, aisled, two porches, tiled roof, Crown Post. 130 ft. long. Brick plinth.	Allowed to fall into ruin but restored in 1985
Widdingon Abbey Barn	c. 1400	Timber frame, tile roof, crown post, weather boarded.	Dept. of the Environment restored in 1983
Cressing Temple Barley Barn	c. 1200	Timber frame. Hipped tile roof with upper vent in small gable. Some of principal posts are 16" in square section. Large porch set midway. Weather boarded. Barn stands on brick plinth with moat to rear.	Essex County Council restored the buildings. Available for education community use.
Wheat Barn	c. 1250	Timber frame. Four equal bays, 130 ft. long, 40 ft. wide and 36 ft. high. Hipped tiled roof. The trusses are some 18 ft. apart. Doors are set midway facing north and south.	In the late 16C the barn was extensively renovated. Timber walls were replaced by brick panels. The whole barn was raised on a brick plinth to restrict rot of the sole plates.
Gloucestershire			
Ashleworth, nr. Glos. Tithe Barn	15th C.	Buttressed stone walls, stone tile roof, two large porches each buttressed, gable end.	Augustinian National Trust
Frocester	c. 1300	Limestone walls, stone slate roof, 13 bays 186ft. X 30ft. 14 buttresses, gable end, two wagon porches on same side.	Benedictine
Stanton	c. 1400	Stone walls, tile roof, six buttresses to side elevation and single porch (midstrey).	Tithe barn near to Church
Hampshire			
Old Basing, Grange Farm Nr. Basingstoke. Tithe barn	c. 1530	Massive brick barn, gable end, 7 brick buttresses, tile roof. Box frame with walls carrying the roof weight. 120 ft. long and 28ft. wide.	Brickwork in English bond Two gothic style entrances between the second and Third and fifth and sixth buttresses. No porch. Now converted to community use.
Titchfield Abbey Tithe Barn	c. 1408	Chalk and flint walls, hipped tiled roof, timber framed. 154ft. long and 37ft. wide. Brick buttresses to end elevations. Two wagon entrances added in 1560. No porch.	Barn has been acquired by the Portsmouth Football Club (2007)

Early English Barns

County Location	Date Built	Construction	Comment
Hereford and Worcester			
Middle Littleton Barn, Evesham	c. 1220	Stone clad barn, stone slate roof, huge gabled stone porch. Stone buttresses to side elevation. Ridge beam and double tie beams. 136ft. long. Base cruck structure.	Benedictine Tithe Barn National Trust
Leigh, Leigh Court Barn Nr. Worcester	c. 1400	Cruck frame (11 pairs) 150ft. X 34ft. tile roof, half hipped. Brick clad with weather boarding. Two large porches.	Nearby are several large square oasts. Tithe barn. Former manor of the Benedictine Abbey of Pershore.
Bredon, nr Tewkesbury	c. 1300	Buttressed cotswold stone walls, stone tile roof, two large porches three stone buttresses to gable. Aisled barn 134ft. by 44ft. Nine bays.	Tithe barn, damaged in 1979 by fire and repaired by National Trust
Kent			
Boxley, nr. Maidstone	c. 1300	Stone barn, tile roof, no porch, gable end with window.	Boxley Abbey lands
Charing, Archbishop's Palace Barn	c. 1300	Stone, tile roof, King Post. 71ft. long and 35ft. wide, double span roof divided by central posts.	Palace c.1300, used as barn from 18th century. An oast kiln was built into one corner
Frindsbury, Rochester	c. 1403	Timber framed, post and truss, vertical boarding, tile roof. Crown post. 210 ft. long, 30 ft. wide.	Recent vandalism (2005) - fire has destroyed one end of barn and part of roof. Church Commissioners own the property.
Littlebourne, nr. Canterbury	1340	Timber framed, post and truss, vertical oak boarding, thatch roof/ water reed has replaced original long straw.	Kentish aisled barn, brick plinth, 172 ft. long divided into 71/2 bays (Originally had nine bays). Barn is aisled on each side and each end. Crown Post roof to collar purlin, arcade posts, many being 16 ins. in square section. (Purchased by Canterbury City Council, 1991 and run by Littlebourne Barn Committee).
Sissinghurst	16th C.	Brick barn, walls carry full weight of the roof, Queen Post.	National Trust
Westenhanger, nr. Folkestone	1528 to 1588	Stone walls, tile roof, two porches, single buttress to gable wall which contains a gothic style window. Fine hammer beam roof to main barn. No aisles.	Restoration in progress (2005). The barn is of L shape
Brook, nr. Wye	1374	Timber framed, post and truss, tile roof, two hipped porches. 120ft. long, six bays, crown post. Barn constructed of English oak.	Manorial barn now used as Wye Agricultural Museum. The site also contains a brick oast house constructed in 1815

County Location	Date Built	Construction	Comment
Kent			
Aylesford Priory, nr. Maidstone, North Barn	18th C.	North barn timber framed. 75 ft long 30ft. wide, no porch, single entrance midstrey. Straw thatch roof.	Barn restored 2005 with Heritage Trust grant of £500,000. Barn has five bays and Queen Post roof.
West Barn	17th C.	Timber framed thatched barn with two wagon porches. Weatherboard clad.	Barn converted for use as cafeteria and bookshop.
London			
Harmondsworth Barn	c 1420	Timber framed aisled barn, post and truss, 192 ft. long with 12 bays stone and brick plinth, tiled roof	Tithe barn, Grade I listed and Scheduled Ancient Monument. In danger due to London airport expansion.
Norfolk			
Hales nr. Beccles	c. 1490	Brick walls carry weight of roof. No vertical posts. Ridge beam and tie beams. Crow stepped gable.	184 feet long with thatched roof
Abbey Farm Barn, Thetford	c. 1440	Eight bay timber framed structure aligned east to west.	Eastern end of barn is dated to 1530 (dendrochronology)
Oxfordshire			
Great Coxwell, Faringdon	1250	Post and truss timber framed barn. Cotswold stone roof (restored 1962). Main arcade posts 22ft. 6ins. high supported on stone plinths 7ft. high. Length 152ft x 44ft. width. Buttressed stone walls and gable. Large stone porch with separate entrance in gable end.	The large gable end door is an 18th addition. Cistercian. National Trust.
Somerset			
Doulting	c. 1400	Stone walls, stone tile roof, no aisles, two large porches each buttressed, gable end buttressed with finial. Eight bays.	One of the Glastonbury Abbey barns (Benedictine).
Bishops Barn, nr. Wells	c. 1400	Buttressed stone walls, slate roof.	
Preston Plucknett	c. 1400	Buttressed stone wall, tile roof, single large stone porch, gable end buttressed with finial. Cruciform ventilation slits.	
Pilton, nr. Glastonbury	c. 1400	Stone Barn. No aisles. Large central porch. Gable ends with cruciform vents. 108ft long and 28ft. wide. Eight bays. East gable has a stone winged man decoration (St. Matthew).	Thatched roof destroyed by fire in 1963. One of the Glastonbury Abbey barns.

Early English Barns

County Location	Date Built	Construction	Comment
Somerset			
Glastonbury Abbey Tithe Barn (Benedictine)	c. 1375	Stone walls, stone tile roof, single large porch to each side. Heavily buttressed, 93ft. long and 33ft. wide. Raised cruck structure.	Agricultural Museum (Somerset Rural Life Museum)
West Pennard Court Barn West Bradley	c. 1400	Stone barn - four buttresses to side elevation tile roof, central porch. Dovecote to one end. Five bays.	National Trust One of the Glastonbury Abbey barns.
Suffolk			
Abbots Hall Barn, Stowmarket		13th century timber framed aisled barn	Museum of East Anglian Life
Leiston Abbey Barn Nr. Aldeburgh	c. 1400	Brick, stone, chalk and flint, Norfolk reed roof, no aisles, tie beam and collar roof.	Located near Abbey ruins
Copdock, nr. Ipswich	c. 1500	Brick barn with crow stepped gables and diaper design brickwork to gable and side walls, ten bays, three massive brick buttresses.	
Abbey Farm Barn, Snape	c. 1400	Timber framed aisled barn. 7 bays, weatherboarded pantiled roof.	Grade II listed/ Serious storm damage in 1987
Wiltshire			
Tisbury Place Farm Barn	c. 1400	Buttressed stone walls 188ft. long and 32ft. wide, 13 bays, Arch braced crucks, collar beams, thatch roof, single porch, two other doors.	Benedictine, Shaftesbury Abbey land. Major alterations in the 15th century
Avebury	c. 1690	Timber framed, post and truss, aisled barn. Thatch roof, 9 bays. 140ft. X 36ft., hip bay at each end, two porches.	Agricultural Museum
Bradford on Avon	c. 1300	Stone walls, stone tile roof, two gabled large porches, each side. Buttresses along length of barn/four buttresses to gable. Cruciform ventilation slits. Raised cruck structure.	Benedictine Former Shaftesbury Abbey land. Barn restored by English Heritage.

Schedule of Illustrated Barns

1. Avebury, Wiltshire
2. Aylesford Priory, Kent
3. Bradford-On-Avon, Wiltshire
4. Doulting, Somerset
5. Glastonbury Abbey, Somerset
6. Great Coxwell, Oxfordshire
7. Littlebourne, Kent
8. Great Dixter, Sussex
9. Coggeshall Abbey, Essex
10. Westenhanger, Kent
11. Cressing Temple, Essex
12. Frindsbury, Rochester, Kent
13. Archbishop's Palace, Charing, Kent
14. Exceat, East Sussex
15. Boxley Abbey (Appendix A)
16. Faversham Abbey (Appendix A)

Avebury, Near Marlborough, Wiltshire

The village of Avebury embraces a complex of 16th and 17th century buildings, a 13th century church (St. James) and the famous megalithic stone circle this latter being a World Heritage Site. Avebury Manor nearby dates from the early 16th century with later alterations. The thatched threshing barn and stable block are 17th century, the dovecote 16th century.

The threshing barn comprises nine bays and measures 140ft, in length and 36 ft. in width. It is a timber framed post and truss aisled structure set upon a low plinth of stone. There are two entrances on each side elevation, the roof is half hipped with small gable and the frame is clad in weatherboard. Internally, the barn has been much altered over time with recycled timbers and heavy metal strapping to joints. Tie-beams set transverse the barn secure the tops of the pairs of principal posts and the feet of principal rafters. Raking struts rise from each side of the tie-beams directly to the principal rafters and act in compression. In discussion with the archaeologists present at the time of my visit in March, 2008, it was confirmed that many of the larger timbers significantly pre-dated the 17th century having been recycled from earlier buildings. The barn now houses a museum with interactive displays relating to the history of the Stone Circle and the Neolithic period (some 6,000 years ago). Archaeological finds are on display in the stable block. The barn is also home to four species of bats.

PLATE 7a: Avebury Barn

Side Elevation of Barn illustrating the two cart doors, hipped/gablet style thatched roof and stone plinth

PLATE 7b: **Avebury Barn**

Side Elevation of Barn illustrating the two cart doors, hipped/gablet style thatched roof and stone plinth

PLATE 8: **Avebury Barn**

Interior carpentry - post and truss timber frame, tie-beam, collar beam, and raking struts. Metal strap work strengthening the joints is clearly evident.

Aylesford Priory (The Friars)

The earliest buildings at the Carmelite Priory date to the 13th century and include the pilgrims' hall, the courtyard, and some part of the cloisters. The main gatehouse is 15th century. The whole complex has been the subject of major conservation works with aid from the Heritage Lottery Fund. The north barn dates from the 18th century and following expenditure of some £500,000 has been saved from dereliction (work completed 2005). The north barn is of post and truss construction with brick plinth. The roof is of straw thatch with Queen Post. Liberal use of metal straps is clearly evident and stainless steel bolts pin major joints but discreetly. Comprising five bays the weather boarded barn is some 75 ft. long and 30 ft. wide. It has a single centrally placed door and is Listed Grade II. Rescued from collapse the barn is now available for a variety of visitor uses and may be hired for events.

A second timber framed and thatched barn on the site (the west barn) has two porches and is used as cafeteria and shop. This barn dates from the 17th century. (Plate 12 - two side elevations of the barn). Aylesford Priory has a complex history and has changed hands many times following dissolution in 1535. More recently it has again become the main house in England for the Carmelite Order and is home to a small community of friars. The priory is an active centre for pilgrimage and prayer.

PLATE 9: **Aylesford Carmelite Priory**
North barn 18th century

PLATE 10: Aylesford Carmelite Priory
Roof carpentry of north barn showing queen posts

Post head joint : illustration of the jowled principal post with longitudinal wall plate, deeply trenched into the post head with transverse tie-beam over. The protruding dowel head indicates where the tie-beam is secured by a mortice framed over a stub tenon cut into the post head. The two upper dowel heads pierce the side of the tie-beam and secure the stub tenon of the principal rafter which is inserted into a mortice cut into the upper face of the tie-beam.

The edge halved scarf joint that extends the wall plate is clearly illustrated and is secured by a face key. Being located directly over the principal post the scarf is well supported (Plate 11).

PLATE 11: **Aylesford Carmelite Priory**
North barn post head joint and edge-halved scarf

PLATE 12: **Aylesford Carmelite Priory**
17th century west barn - two elevations

PLATE 12: **Aylesford Carmelite Priory**
17th century west barn - two elevations

Bradford on Avon Tithe Barn, Wiltshire

The tithe barn at Bradford-on-Avon has been dated to the early 14th century being built as part of a medieval farmstead belonging to Shaftesbury Abbey. The barn is located within the ancient town of Bradford-on-Avon a short distance from the bridge and church. English Heritage has responsibility for the barn's conservation. The stone barn is covered with a stone tiled roof, is 167 ft. in length, 30 ft. in width and has fourteen bays. There are no aisles. It lies on an east to west axis. There are two large stone porches standing out from the north and the south elevations. Each is gabled and those on the north side have cruciform ventilation slits and decorative finials at the ridge. A small door in the side wall of the porch provides ease of access. Across the width of the barn between the pairs of porch doors are stone threshing floors.

The roof carpentry is of the highest quality and quite dramatic. The structure is a raised base cruck with some bays being of two tiered crucks the upper being set upon a collar beam that secures the tops of the pairs of lower cruck blades. Other cruck frames are continuous to the ridge. Collar beams are strengthened by arched bracing from below. Purlins further strengthen the roof and are trenched into the cruck blades of the lower and upper frames. The base of each of the pairs of cruck blades is set fully into the thick stone walls of the barn some seven feet above ground level and stand upon wooden blocks that operate as a wall plate as well as resisting penetration of ground moisture rising through the stone to rot the structural timbers. The full weight of the roof is carried on the crucks and transferred down to the barn walls which are strong enough to carry the huge compression forces and which are heavily buttressed to counteract the outward thrust.

PLATE 13: **Bradford on Avon**

North side elevation of the tithe barn illustrating the gabled porches, small gothic style entrance in the porch wall and the heavy stone buttressing.

PLATE 14: **Bradford on Avon**
Roof carpentry with raised base crucks set into the stone walls of the barn. The cavernous internal space is well evident.

PLATE 15: **Bradford on Avon**

Close-up view of upper cruck and collar beam with trenched purlins.

PLATE 16: **Bradford on Avon**
Stone threshing floor across the barn with between porch doors.

Doulting, Near Glastonbury, Somerset

Situated some ten miles from Glastonbury Abbey. Doulting barn is one of four surviving stone barns of the many which were spread throughout the Abbey's vast estates. Others nearby include the Cumhill barn at Pilton (14th century) damaged by fire in 1963 and the smaller 15th century Court barn at West Pennard/West Bradley. Other barns are thought to have been lost over time as they fell into disrepair or were plundered for their stone for use in other buildings. The Doulting barn remains in use as a farm building today and is dated to circa 1400. An earlier date of 1275 has been proposed but I have not been able to substantiate this. The barn has substantial stone walls, a stone tiled roof and no aisles. The two buttressed cart porches reach out from each side elevation and provide good access with two threshing floor areas set in the width of the barn between each of the two pairs of doors. The presence of the two cart porches however is estimated to reduce the available internal storage area by a quarter. The barn has eight bays.

PLATE 77: Doulting Barn

With its two huge gabled porches is set within a large farmyard area bounded on two sides by stone walls and faced by a range of smaller farm buildings. Note the pedestrian entrance into the barn via a gothic style door set into the side of the stone porch.

Glastonbury Abbey Tithe Barn, Somerset

Records indicate the existence of a church on this site dating from the 7th century and by the Conquest (1066) the wealthy Abbey owned vast areas of the surrounding land as well as large estates in Wiltshire, Hampshire, Berkshire, Devon and Dorset. The town of Glastonbury grew up around the Benedictine Abbey and it was the monks who began the draining of the Somerset levels to bring more land into agriculture. Large flocks of sheep, valuable for their wool, were grazed on the extensive pasture land. Crop rotation was practiced on the arable land growing wheat, oats, barley for malting as the main ingredient for brewing ale. The Abbey's farm was some 524 acres by the mid thirteenth century and some land was let to tenants and tithes were collected.

The tithe barn occupies an area to the south-east corner of what was the 36 acre walled precinct surrounding the now ruined Abbey. The barn is a substantial stone structure and was built circa 1375. It is 93 ft. in length and 33 ft. in width with seven bays and no aisles. The roof timbers are mainly oak but with some elm and chestnut. Dendrochronology dating of the roof timbers in 1978-80 indicate felling dates in the early to middle years of the 14th century. Manorial records indicate the repair of a thatched barn on the site in 1302-3 with further thatch repairs in 1333-34. Records exist of roofing with stone tiles in 1389-90. The stone walls of the barn are over three feet thick and are mainly of dressed limestone with some marl stone and blue lias. Huge gabled wagon porches are set midstrey to either side elevation , barn walls and porch are heavily buttressed. Decorative details include elaborate stone carvings to the gables of barn and porch, trefoil window in the barn gable and cruciform vents, and a rectangular window in the porch gable. Internally the roof carpentry is of a two-tiered cruck system with eight pairs of cruck blades rising from halfway up the stone walls each pair joined at their top by a collar beam which in turn is strengthened from below by arch braces. Set on top of the collars and the plate are a second pair of cruck blades rising to the ridge and secured to each other midway by a short tie beam. Upper and lower crucks each carry a heavy purlin running the length of the barn. Substantial arched wind braces strengthen the roof by stiffening the purlins, cruck blades and plate.

Somerset County Council has restored and conserved the barn and in the 1970's repaired and renewed much of the roof timber. In 1978 Cotswold stone tiles were used to replace the roof material. The barn forms part of the Somerset Rural Life Museum and houses displays of farm equipment and machinery.

PLATE 19: **Glastonbury Abbey Tithe Barn**
Decorative stonework to barn gable (west end) illustrating trefoil window, cruciform vents and carved stone image of an eagle, the symbol of St. John.

PLATE 18: Glastonbury Abbey Tithe Barn
Side Elevation of the barn showing decorative work to porch gable

PLATE 20: Glastonbury Abbey Tithe Barn

Roof carpentry illustrating the two-tier cruck structure.

PLATE 21: **Glastonbury Abbey Tithe Barn**
Arched wind braces.

Great Coxwell, Near Faringdon, Oxfordshire

The Manor of Faringdon was granted by King John to the Cistercian Abbey of Beaulieu in 1204 and it was the monks (probably lay brothers) who built the stone clad barn at Great Coxwell circa 1250. The barn is a huge magnificent structure standing well clear of Faringdon in open but sloping windswept fields. It is considered by many to be unrivalled in its splendour by any of the existing medieval barns in this country.

The barn measures 152 ft. in length, 44ft in width with a ridge height of 48ft. and is set on a north to south axis. There are huge stone porches to the east and west side elevations and these entrances were supplemented in the 18th century by even larger doors set into the gable walls at each end of the barn. Structurally the barn is a timber framed post and truss aisled building clad with Cotswold stone with ashlar faced buttresses. The roof is covered with Cotswold stone tiles having been renewed by the National Trust in the early 1960's. The roof carpentry is delightful. Six transverse frames create a seven bay interior. The principal oak posts are 22ft. 6ins. tall and are set upon tall stone bases (pillars) some 7ft. high which are capped with oak plates to resist rising ground moisture. Tie beams set under the arcade plates secure the tops of the pairs of principal posts to help strengthen the frame and the feet of principal rafters tenoned into the outer ends of these ties are thereby prevented from spreading.

An unusual feature is the elbow shaped struts (Queen Posts) rising from the tie-beams to principal rafters to prevent their inward sag and therefore acting in compression. Heavy roof purlins run the length of the barn and the tops of the rafters are secured by the ridge beam (purlin). The National Trust is the custodian of the barn being responsible for its conservation.

PLATE 22: **Great Coxwell Barn**
Side elevation of the tithe barn illustrating the huge stone porch with pedestrian entrance to the side wall and buttressed gable end with 18th century door opening.

PLATE 23: Great Coxwell Barn
Interior of the barn illustrating the central nave and lines of principal posts set upon stone pillars. The heavy bracing to the tie-beams is clearly evident. Similarly the elbow shaped Queen posts supporting the rafters.

PLATE 24: **Great Coxwell Barn**
Illustrates the ties from the principal posts to the wall plate with bracket supports standing upon stone corbels.

PLATE 25: **Great Coxwell Barn**
Gable end illustrating 18th century door, ventilation slits and heavy stone buttresses. An indication of scale is given by reference to the saloon car adjacent to the boundary wall.

Littlebourne Barn

This is one of the best surviving examples of 14th century timber framed barns in England. Dating from 1340 the barn stands on land owned at that time by St. Augustine's Abbey in Canterbury. The barn is 172 ft. long with 7 ½ bays (it originally had 9 bays) and is aisled on all four sides. The barn stands upon a low brick wall protecting the timber from damp rot. The cladding is of vertical oak boards. The crown post roof is now covered in water reed, the original having been long straw. Two reed thatched porches were added to the barn in 1961.

The barn was purchased by Canterbury City Council in 1991 and is now under the day to day management of the Littlebourne Barn Committee. It serves the local community as a venue for social events, visiting groups, weddings, etc. Adjacent to the barn is the 13th century flint towered church of St. Vincent. Other buildings on the site which appeared on the 1842 tithe map included a granary and circular oast house but these have long since gone.

PLATE 26: **Littlebourne Barn**
Side elevation

PLATE 27: **Littlebourne Barn**
Wagon door, framed ledged and braced.

Early English Barns

PLATE 28: **Littlebourne Barn**
Roof carpentry with Crown Post (two views). Note vertical board cladding

PLATE 29: **St. Vincent's Church**
13th century sited adjacent to the barn

Great Dixter

Situated at Northiam in the Sussex Weald the renowned gardens of the late Christopher Lloyd include a charming house dating, in part, from the mid 15th century. The house has a timber framed great hall measuring 40 ft. by 25 ft. and 31 ft. high with hammer beams strengthened by a tie beam. It appears the Hall originally had a centrally sited open fire from which smoke exited through a hole in the roof and unglazed (but shuttered) windows, The roof beams still reveal the sooty black deposits. The house has been enlarged and altered many times over its long life. In the splendid gardens that entirely surround the house is a large timber framed barn with a block of three square brick oast kilns at one end.

The barn is weather boarded and its large tiled roof sweeps down to within five feet of the ground on the garden side. The cavernous internal space has five large tie beams traversing the timber frame to the wall plates each beam having a king post at its centre. There are no aisles. The king posts act in extension to prevent any tendency to sag in the tie beams and each of these posts is anchored by a metal rod piercing through the beam and secured on the underside of the beam by a metal plate to resist withdrawal. The tie beams are massive timbers each representing a single tree but squared for use. Two purlins run the length of the roof on each side giving support to the common rafters. Two large doors are sited along the side elevation but no porch or canopy. No date is given for the barn but it is claimed to be of similar date to the house. However the ridge and king post suggest it was much more recent. The oast comprises three large square kilns, clay tiled roofs and with cowls intact. They were built around 1890. Local hops were dried in the kilns up to 1939. The barn is now used for storage purposes at one end, the other being utilised as a craft workshop where a carpenter/joiner is making garden furniture using Dixter wood.

PLATE 30: **Great Dixter**
Barn and oast kilns

PLATE 31: **Great Dixter**
Barn Roof Carpentry – King Post

Coggeshall Abbey- The Grange Barn

The Savignac Abbey founded in 1142 at Coggeshall was absorbed by the Cistercian Order in 1147 as with all other Savignac monasteries. The resident choir monks were priests whose life was purely spiritual and contemplative, the work on the grange being the responsibility of the lay brothers who, in addition to providing agricultural labour had within their number many of the crafts including that of carpentry, masonry, milling and many other skills essential to the running of the Abbey and farm. The Abbey was destroyed in the mid 16th century at the dissolution but the ruins remain. Comprising six bays the Grange barn is a substantial timber framed, post and truss aisled building some 130 ft. long with two hipped porches, weatherboard cladding and a tiled half hipped roof. This latter is thought to date from the 14th century prior to which the roof would have been straw thatch or reed. The outer timbers stand upon a low brick wall and the arcade posts rest upon stone/concrete pads. Extensive rebuilding was undertaken in the 14th century but the principal posts which were originally set upon timber baulks survive from the early barn.

The roof of the barn is of Crown post configuration supporting a collar purlin which runs the length of the roof. The crown posts are braced by diagonal timbers tenoned into the massive transverse tie beams. After falling into a derelict condition with half the roof and two bays collapsed in the 1970's the barn was eventually restored in the mid 1980's following considerable lobbying and fund raising by the Grange Barn Trust and with the help of Braintree District Council and the

Manpower Services Commission. The barn passed to the National Trust in 1989. Originally held to date from the 15th century radiocarbon analysis in 1976 recorded a date for the principal posts of 1020 plus or minus 90 years. Subsequent dendrochronology dating techniques in 1994 provided a "felling date" for the oldest timbers of 1237 - 70 and mid 13th century is now the accepted date for the barn. As such it is one of the oldest timber framed barns in Europe.

PLATE 32: **The Grange Barn**
Front elevation of Coggeshall barn with two wagon porches, and hipped roof with gablet

PLATE 33: The Grange Barn
Roof carpentry with Crown Post

PLATE 34: The Grange Barn
Edge Halved Scarf Joint

The following is taken from a display at the Coggeshall barn :

ON DIVIDING THE CORN HARVEST

One part cast forth, for rent due out of hand.

One other part for seed to sow thy land.
Another part leave parson for his tythe.

Another part for harvest, sickle and scythe.

One part for plough-wright, Cartwright, knacker and Smith.

One part, to uphold teams that draw therewith.
One part for servant, and workman's wages lay.

One part, likewise for fill-belly, day by day.
One part thy wife, nor needful things doth crave.
Thyself and thy child, the last one part would have.

Thomas Tusser (1524 - 80)
Five Hundred Points of Good Husbandry (1557)

Westenhanger Castle and Barns (Kent)

The present castle buildings are the remains of a fortified 14th century quadrangular house. The building has considerable history. The medieval barn complex was built between 1528 and 1588 and constructed primarily of Kentish ragstone with some Caen stone imported from Normandy. The walls of the barn are over 3 ft. thick. The barn is 120 ft. long, has eleven bays and an internal span of 25ft. 7 ins. with a pair of wagon porches projecting from each of the east and west sidewalls. The hammer beam roof is of oak. The structure straddles the East Stour stream which has been carefully culverted by means of a two centred barrel-vaulted brick culvert beneath the barn. The barn roof suffered substantial damage in the great storm of 1987 and consequent exposure of the structure led to further deterioration. The barn outbuilding complex is comprised of the vast main barn (the Smythe barn) with a stone stable and storage range running from it at right angles. This second building is 140 ft. long and 20 ft. wide and is thought to date from circa 1525. Many of the doors and window openings are surrounded by cut and carved stonework thought to have been re-used from the former church of St. John which was deconsecrated in circa 1450 but of which there is now no trace on the site.

At the time of my visit to the site with the Kent and Surrey Regional Group of the SPAB (May, 2007 and September. 2008) a substantial temporary roof covering was in place over the main barn with considerable scaffolding around the structure. A survey of the repairs required to restore the barn had been completed and grant aid of £500,000 awarded by English Heritage. Work on the repair of the hammerbeam roof was in progress by a small team of carpenters. All the roof tiles (some 50,000) had been removed and stored on site. The repair, replacement or strengthening of the great oak timbers was in progress. To ensure as much original timber was retained as possible the carpenters were using an unusual technique which involved gouging sections of wood from the badly decayed timbers and replacing it with new oak inserted into the gouged cavity being secured by an epoxy resin glue and pinned with dowel pegs. This provided the essential strengthening of the timber without replacing it and the visual effect from below was of untreated timber since the grafting or splicing in of the new wood was carried out from the upper facing surface. Other rafters and bracing pieces had tenoned ends replaced with new oak skilfully jointed into the old oak timbers. This time-consuming work requiring great care and precision will be a lasting testimony to the considerable skill and knowledge of timber of the carpenters concerned.

PLATE 35: **Westenhanger Castle Barn**

Picture of Hammerbeam Roof prior to commencement of repairs. The hammer beam brackets are mounted upon stone corbels.

PLATE 36: Westenhanger Castle Barn
Gable-end of the stables and storage barn which join to and run at right angles from the main barn.

Early English Barns | 119

PLATE 37: **Westenhanger Castle Barn**
Side view illustrating the worked stone around the door and window openings (two views)

PLATE 38. Westenhanger Castle Barn
Repaired arch-braced Hammerbeam.

Cressing Temple: Wheat And Barley Barns

Standing within a farm complex on the former Cressing estate in Essex are two large medieval timber framed aisled barns that date to the 13th century. The long history of the land at Cressing includes occupation by the religious order, the Knights Templar, in the 12th century. They farmed the arable lands to raise money for their Order and to finance the crusades. The Pope disbanded the Order in 1312 and the manor of Cressing passed to another religious order the Knights Hospitaller. At the dissolution of the monasteries Henry VIII suppressed that Order and confiscated the buildings and lands. Since then the properties have passed through many secular ownerships. In 1987 Essex County Council with financial aid from English Heritage and the National Heritage Memorial Fund purchased Cressing Temple to safeguard the site for posterity and it now enjoys scheduled Ancient Monument status. The site comprises a substantial agricultural visitor centre and the barns are utilised for conferences, education purposes and large community events.

The Wheat Barn

Built by the Knights Templar to store their corn in about 1260. The barn is of timber frame with aisles, it has four equal bays and the ends of the barns are cantilevered. The barn is set on an east/west axis and is some 130ft. long, 40ft. wide and 36 ft high. Records indicate it was built from 472 oak trees and dendrochronology indicates felling dates between 1257 and 1290. The six trusses are set 18ft. apart and the arcade posts are made from complete tree trunks. The main doors face north and south, one side having a large wagon porch with hipped roof, the other a canopy roof. Originally the barn walls were constructed of vertical oak planks set between two studs per bay, however over time and particularly as a consequence of major repairs in the late 16th century the whole barn was raised onto a low brick plinth wall to prevent rot of the sole plates and the wall planking was replaced by brick panels. The roof is clay tiled and both the wheat and barley barns were re-roofed in 1988-89 following substantial damage caused by the great gales of 1987. (Plate 39)

The Barley Barn

Built about 1200-1220 from 480 oak trees. Dendrochronology provides felling dates between 1205 and 1235. Mr. C. Hewett comments that in 1956 six samples of timber were taken from various positions in the barn and subjected to radiocarbon (C 14) isotope analysis and the assessed age was 1200 plus or minus sixty years. The barn is some 117 ft. long, 44ft. wide and 37ft. high. It was originally longer and wider but major repairs in the 14th century resulted in wall replacement inside the line of the original and the loss of half of one bay. Further repairs in about 1500 introduced the crown post roof with collars and purlins. The arcade posts are transversely joined by two tie beams one above the other and these principal posts divide the barn into four equal bays.

The clay tiled roof has a gablet in the small gable intended to aid ventilation. Barn walls were originally of wooden boards succeeded by wattle and daub panels but this was later weather boarded. Internal walls are of lathe and plaster. Like the wheat barn, the barley barn has been raised off the ground and set onto a low brick plinth. A hipped porch door is centrally situated (midstrey) in the side elevation. The barley barn is illustrated at Plate 41 and the post and truss framing at Plate 42.

Early English Barns | 123

PLATE 39: **The Wheat Barn**

shows the north and south elevation of the wheat barn. The large porch and opposite canopy doors, and the brick panels are clearly shown together with the brick plinth.

PLATE 40: **The Wheat Barn** shows the wheat barn roof carpentry. The remains of scissor bracing can be seen lapped across the principal posts, tie beam and collar beam rising to the principal rafters on the opposite side of the barn

PLATE 41: **The Barley Barn**
The Barley Barn (1200)

PLATE 42: The Barley Barn

Roof Structure

Frindsbury Barn, Manor Farm, Rochester

Frindsbury lies within the Medway District of Kent the land being formerly a demesne of St. Andrew of Rochester. The timber framed post and truss barn is 210 ft. long, 30 ft. wide, is set on a north-south axis and has a crown post roof with thirteen bays. It is dated to circa 1300. Mr. C. Hewett refers (English Historic Carpentry) to a radiocarbon date of AD 1400 plus or minus 60. The isotope laboratory tests were undertaken by Professors Horn and Berger (Radiocarbon 1968 No. 410).

The building is owned by the Church Commissioners and was used for agricultural storage purposes until recent times. In 2002 fire caused damage to the roof and again sometime in January, 2003 when three bays were severely burned and the roof partly exposed to the weather. Remarkably the principal posts, although surface charred, remained sound. At that time the Church Commissioners with some financial aid from the SPAB had a metal security fence erected around the barn and English Heritage and the Commissioners continue to seek potential uses for the structure that will retain its form for posterity. Plate 43 illustrates the barn following installation of the security fence and the photographs were taken during a visit to the site with the SPAB Regional Group in May, 2003.

PLATE 43: Frindsbury Barn
Rochester (1403)

PLATE 44: **Ffindsbury Barn**
Crown Post Roof, Tie Beam, Post and Plate in "Normal" Assembly

PLATE 45: **Frindsbury Barn**
Wall Tie, Post and Plate in "Reversed" Assembly

The Crown post roof, arch bracing and jowl posts are clearly presented at Plate 44. The arcade plate is framed into the head of the jowled arcade post. The tie beam is framed over the plate and jowl post in what is termed "normal assembly". Horizontal struts and vertical struts sit within the spandrels (space between jowl and transverse arch brace) acting to strengthen the frame. The lower wall plate at the eaves of the barn is in "reversed assembly" since the longitudinal plate rests on top of the tie beam and is not framed into the head of the wall post . Refer to Plate 45. This photograph also shows a passing shore half lapped into the aisle tie beam. It rises diagonally from the outer end of the groundsill to strengthen the head of the arcade post. Plate 46 illustrates the stop splayed (cut obliquely) scarf joint with face key used to join sections of thick wall plate timbers in order to create the longitudinal timber extending the length of the barn. Edge to edge vertical plank boarding encloses the frame of the barn. As recorded by Mr. S. Rigold (Archaeologica Cantiana p. 11) "both aisle plate and sole plate have

Early English Barns | 131

grooves stopped at the halfway stud and in these are fitted edge to edge vertical planks an inch thick, each one pegged to the half height rail. The cladding cannot be renewed without displacing the aisle plates which in turn, cannot be removed without displacing the aisle rafters which are housed over them". In consequence it seems we may take the view that such vertical planking is the original.

More recently it was sad to learn that on the 14th February, 2006, yet a further fire had occurred at the barn this time to the opposite end of the structure from that of the fire of January, 2003. The flames penetrated the area toward the end of the roof and the structure is now further exposed to the elements. The full extent of the damage is not yet known. N.B. Cornerstone (SPAB) 2008 : Dendrochronolgy analysis of the barn timbers has reassessed its date at A.D. 1403.

PLATE 46: **Frindsbury Barn**
Stop Splayed Scarf Joint

The Archbishop's Palace, Charing, Kent

This medieval palace may seem out of place in a book on barns and oasthouses but it is considered worthy of inclusion since for over two hundred years the Great Hall, built circa 1300 was used as a barn and at the south eastern end within the barn an oast has been constructed. The building featured in the BBC's television Restoration programme and at the time of my visit to the site in June, 2005, with the SPAB Regional Group urgent repair work to the stone wall at the northern end of the Great Hall was imminent since it was in danger of collapse. The local Trust is seeking grant aid to conserve the building for potential community use.

The series of buildings that comprise the remains of the Palace are scheduled Ancient Monuments being Grade I listed. The manor of Charing is recorded as a possession of the see of Canterbury from the 8th century and the Palace stands adjacent to the parish church of St. Peter and St. Paul. The five bay Hall was converted for use as a barn in the 18th century. It is some 71 ft. long and 35 ft. wide. The original roof was a single span but when it was re-roofed the pitch was reduced and the roof constructed in two spans divided by central posts. The walls are of stone. The roof is covered with clay tiles and the double height door in the west elevation has a canopy.

As can be expected the building has been much altered in its long life with many additions and alteration including strengthening of the stone with brick. The re-roofing in reduced pitch involved the introduction of central posts carrying an arcade plate running the length of the hall and this provides support for the rafters for the two span roof. The tie beams traverse the width of the hall and cross on top of the central plate at the junction with the posts. Bracing is from each side of the central posts to tie beams by means of mortice and tenon joints and again from post to centre plate.

PLATE 47: **Charing Archbishop's Palace Barn**
The Great Hall c.1300 (western elevation)

PLATE 48: **Charing Archbishop's Palace Barn**
Roof Structure - two views detailing central posts, tie beams, central arcade plate and bracing. The King Posts are common to each of the roof spans.

Exceat : East Sussex County Council - Seven Sisters Country Park

The main Sussex barn has been converted for use as a visitor centre for the Seven Sisters Country Park. The flint barn was built in the eighteenth century and is part of an interconnected complex of flint built buildings which include a second barn also used in conjunction with the Country Park activities.

The main barn is of timber frame. The jowled oak posts twelve inches in square section form an aisle on one side of the barn. The walls are of flint and the natural slope of the ground provides for a split level floor space, the lower area being formerly a stable for horses and cattle. There is one central entrance but no porch. The walls have flint buttresses whilst the secondary buildings have heavy brick buttresses. The roof is hipped at one end and half-hipped at the other. It is covered with clay tiles.

PLATE 49: Exceat Barn, East Sussex
Barn front elevation

Early English Barns | 137

PLATE 50: **Exceat Barn, East Sussex**
Side elevation of the building complex

PLATE 51: **Exceat Barn, East Sussex**
Roof carpentry of the main barn

CHAPTER **2**

An Introduction to Methods of Dating Timber Framed Barns

- (i) Historical Records
- (ii) Radiocarbon Analysis
- (iii) Dendrochronology

2   Methods of Dating Timber Framed Barns

The process of dating old buildings, let alone a timber framed barn, is complex and a wide range of indicators, including construction features, need to be considered. The assessment will prudently be undertaken with great care and focus upon detail within a framework of scientifically and technically accepted methods linked to and including detailed reference to proven historical documents and records including parish, manorial and estate records. The many examples of barn structures encompassed by this book cover a wide range of building dates from the early medieval granges and tithe barns to more recent structures, in all extending over some six hundred years from 12th century to the 18th century. L. F. Salzman recommends "that no attempt should be made to date a building until search has been made for documentary evidence bearing upon it. Even documentary evidence requires careful handling and it is first essential to be sure that the building in question is that referred to by the chronicler and has not been rebuilt".

In researching particular structures and sites necessarily involving site visits, local records and published articles and books it occurred to me there were considerable challenges in determining relatively accurate dates for the older timber framed barns and the following are examples of the complications encountered.

(i)   Significant structural changes and major repairs may have been made to the timber framed barn over its long life, in particular, re-roofing (new timbers, thatch replaced by tile), perhaps the building of outshots and porches, and the addition or deletion of bays quite apart from replacement of rotted timbers or the inclusion of further bracing for strength. Where the re-modelling and repairs are of major significance the decision of dating can, in my view, become a matter of conjecture. As an analogy we may consider a veteran motor car - at what stage in the renewal and rebuilding of such an historic vehicle e.g. renewal of chassis, coachwork, engine, etc. does the integrity of the original structure and mechanics become lost. In practice there has been resort to the Courts of Law to determine the legitimacy of vendors' claims of vehicle antiquity e.g. recent controversy over the sale of a vintage supercharged Bentley "Blower" for the sum of one million pounds. In the context of the timber framed barn therefore the assessment of date must balance the question and magnitude of change.

(ii) Whereas historical records and maps may enable the site of a barn to be clearly identified and give positive indications regarding date and use the original timber structure may at some stage have suffered severe fire damage with a new building subsequently being erected on the same site. Historical records therefore may refer to a barn at a particular location but is it the same barn today? Examination for any re-alignment at the site may provide a clue as to whether a new structure exists.

(iii) Re-use of the massive timber posts, beams and rafters is widely acknowledged and can be evidenced by the presence of exposed unused mortices in the post timbers, or oversized mortices in beams where different widths of tenons in braces or struts fail to fully engage in the original mortice. Evidence of unused lap joints may also be present in the form of vacant trenches. Radiocarbon dating of samples of particular timbers may not in such cases reflect the date of the barn but merely the date of the timbers examined.

(iv) One final complication relates to the nature of timber samples taken for radiocarbon dating. The technical evaluation in the isotope laboratory has to take into account the position from which the sample of wood was extracted from the timber post or beam. Clearly a major oak timber will have been hewn from a tree of considerable age, say 200 years or more. Therefore a sample of wood taken from the outer (newer) growth rings of the timber will be of significantly different age from that taken from the older growth near the central rings of the tree. A variance of 100 years or more could result. I comment later on radiocarbon degradation concepts and the nature of other variables.

Where then do we start the process of attempting to date a structure. We need to draw upon the widest range of material, historical documentation and scientific analysis. The National Archives at Kew include the Public Records Office and the Historical Manuscripts Commission records. Research will commence with a careful examination of local historical records, county or parish records, estate records, ecclesiastical records, maps, etc. Local historical societies and archaeological groups may each provide useful material that helps to identify the barn, its history and function in the context of local agricultural life. Tithe maps were produced between 1838 and 1854 but most were based upon much earlier surveys and estate documents. The latter generally include information on tenancies, rents and leases, land surveys and title deeds. A national farm survey was undertaken in 1941-43 which includes a description of every farm with details of crops, livestock, labour and buildings. An earlier survey was undertaken in 1910 with a view to imposing a tax on land. It required a description of farm properties and acreages.

    Moving forward the next criteria to be evaluated should include the nature of the carpentry jointing that binds together the great timbers forming the frame of the barn, in particular the principal posts and trusses, tie beams and roof structure, scarf jointing of the wall plates and the nature of the external cladding. Vertical boards are generally an indication of an earlier date than horizontal boards (e.g. Frindsbury barn at Rochester).   Extensive research of medieval timber jointing was undertaken by Mr. Cecil Hewett, an acknowledged expert on medieval carpentry. He sets out in his book "English Historic Carpentry" a highly technical exposition of historic structural carpentry heavily illustrated with detailed case studies of specific timber frames and jointing techniques, in particular, his research embraced cathedrals, abbeys and other church roofs, belfrys, towers, spires and many medieval barns the latter including considerable work in Essex, in particular Cressing Temple wheat and barley barns and at Coggeshall. These researches illustrate and trace the differences in styles of jointing and assembling of timber frames over time. The proposition is developed that since "carpenters' jointing techniques had of necessity to attain mechanical efficiency if their structures were to endure for any length of time" then jointing techniques would progressively develop such that, despite a great variety of framework styles each period of time would be characterised by definite assembly methods as carpenters sought to improve the mechanical efficiency of the joints. It is argued the above analysis is intended to provide indictors for dating particular timber frames and indeed it is generally accepted that ridge beams were not a feature of the earliest barns in southern England and as previously stated vertical board cladding generally pre-dates horizontal cladding, the latter requiring more sophisticated sawing techniques to ensure boards could butt together or later to be feathered for overlapping. Mr. Hewett asserts that the scarfing of timbers into long top plates was perfected by the last decade of the 13th century and the reader is urged to examine further the variations in scarfing over time as detailed in Mr. Hewett's book. Forms of post head jointing and tie beam lap joints etc. and joints for framing floors, moulding and roof designs each play their part in the determination of possible dates. However, the transition between one set of carpentry joint to the new must have evolved over a lengthy period of time and clearly it cannot be assessed when older jointing systems might have passed out of use as new more effective joints were developed. It cannot reasonably be envisaged that any one structure will incorporate each of the most efficient forms of the many categories of joints. Inevitably it will be a mixture of old and new.

It is worthy of note that detailed carpentry research by Mr. Hewett at the Cressing Temple medieval barley barn was instrumental in the re-dating of the barn from 1480 to 1200 and the wheat barn to 1255 dates later confirmed by carbon 14 dating techniques in the 1960s. While it is recognised that developments in carpentry over time provide an added tool in the complex problem of dating old timber framed buildings there remains a strong body of opinion that seeks substantial further research of other building structures particularly on a more widely based sample and geographical spread before acceptance of that technique can be universal. The carefully structured work and analysis by Mr. Hewett does however provide an additional and tangible source of historical evidence which should help, with other records and techniques, the determination of probable dates or a range of probabilities within closely defined parameters.

Radiocarbon Dating

The science of radiocarbon dating was first developed by W.F Libby, the American physicist, in 1946/1947. The development and gradual sophistication of radiocarbon dating (carbon 14) has provided scientific accuracy to the evaluation processes referred to above. A technical explanation of this scientific method is set out in the book "Scientific Methods in Medieval Archaeology" (edited by Rainer Berger) being a series of papers presented at an International Conference held at the University of California in October, 1967. See also the bibliography.

The method of radiocarbon dating is technically complex with the testing process requiring particular care both in sample selection, cleaning away pollutants and sample preparation prior to the detailed isotope laboratory analysis including high precision accelerator mass spectrometer techniques. As such it is a relatively expensive exercise. The principle underlying the dating method postulates that the proportion of the unstable radiocarbon 14 isotope to stable C12 isotope has remained constant over the past 50,000 years. A timber post being examined for dating had therefore a similar radiocarbon content many hundreds of years ago when it was a living tree as the level of radiocarbon in current day living trees. Therefore it is the degree of decline (decay) in radiocarbon content since the tree was felled that has to be calculated in order to date the sample. Carbon 14 decays at a known constant rate, half the C14 being lost over 5,730 years..

Plant growth is dependent upon the phenomena of photosynthesis during which the plants absorb radiocarbon from carbon dioxide in the atmosphere. In the context of tree growth, once the sapwood of the new growth converts into heartwood it ceases to take up any more radiocarbon and as a consequence the carbon 14 cycle of decay begins. Similarly upon the death of a plant (felling of the tree) the degradation of carbon 14 in the whole tree begins. It will be evident therefore that in a tree of some 100-200 years of age the carbon 14 content of a sample extracted from the outer edge of the trunk (younger growth) will vary from a sample extracted from heartwood nearer to the central (earlier) growth rings. This variable is one of the adjustments to be considered in determining and fine tuning the date of a particular timber post or beam. However the crucial data remains the determination of the felling date.

Following from the above criterion, the carbon 14 assessment compares the residual amount of radiocarbon present in the wood sample taken from the timber post or beam to be dated with the known present day carbon yardstick. The difference between these two determines the quantum of C 14 decay that has occurred. This is then compared with the known decay rate of carbon 14 to yield the amount of time passed, thereby dating the timber within assessed tolerances expressed as plus/minus to provide an effective range. The process is further sophisticated by considering and where appropriate making adjustments for proven variables: e.g. fossil fuels, increased carbon in the atmosphere in the 19th and 20th centuries but is considered irrelevant for dating medieval samples and similarly nuclear testing pollution. Solar flare activity does affect radiocarbon levels through changes in cosmic rays reaching the atmosphere (thesis by H. E. Suess). A conversion table called the Calibration Curve has been developed for the period 800 AD to 1900 AD that modifies the C 14 dates for this constancy variation.

Research published in February, 2006, records further advances in radiocarbon dating utilising oxygen isotope levels found in the Greenland ice core, amongst others, which have resulted in the further modification of the calibration curve. The consequence is that some hitherto established dates are proven to be significantly earlier than previously thought. The research was directed toward large archaeological time scales of 30,000 years or more. However, the consequences for the comparatively short time scales with which we are concerned in the dating of timbers is considered to have only a marginal effect upon the assessed date range but essentially reinforcing the earlier end of that given range. Whilst there is generally a close proximity between radiocarbon 14 determined dates and dates determined by dendrochronology, scientific analysis has proved that a small change in carbon 14 levels has occurred over past centuries for which a correction factor (calibration adjustment) is required.

Examples of carbon 14 dating (C. Hewett - English Historic Carpentry).

1. Paul's Hall Barn, Belchamp St. Paul, Essex

    The derelict barn circa 1200 is the last of three built on the site and is aligned north to south. Carbon 14 analysis of an earth based post standing on a lime cement pad in the south west angle of the barn indicated as follows: the determined age was 924 years plus or minus 95 years before A.D. 1950. The central date was A.D. 1026 and the date range 931 to 1121.

2. Cressing Temple Barley Barn, Essex

    Six samples of timber were taken from various parts of the barn in 1956 and the determined age was A.D. 1200 plus or minus 60 years. The central date was therefore A.D. 1200 and the date range 1140 to 1260. The analysis was undertaken by Professor Berger and Professor Horn of California.

Dendrochronology

The science of dendrochronology provides arguably the primary method of dating the great timbers used in the construction and framing of barns. Dates assessed for particular (13th, 14th and 15th century) timbers can and have been cross checked with radiocarbon (carbon 14) samples and subject to minor adjustments of the latter the correlation provides a high level of confidence. It remains however for the assessor to interpret this factual evidence in the wider context of the particular barn structure e.g. the extent the specific timber is original to the barn under examination or is a re-used timber from an earlier building.

Dendrochronology is the study of the sequence of the annual growth rings in trees to determine a record of dates (the years in which each tree ring grew) thereby calculating the age of the tree and codifying the physical nature of each growth ring i.e. wide or narrow. The ability to determine such dates and construction of growth ring profiles enables cross matching to other timbers over a long timescale and helps the process of clarifying evolutionary trends in structure type. Much work has been done in building a master tree ring chronology, particularly for oak trees, covering many hundreds of years and certainly pre-dating the 11th century which adequately encompasses the period with which we are concerned. Plate 52 illustrates concentric tree rings in a cross section of timber. The outer cambian tissue is well defined being the divide between the formation of layers of new wood tissue on its inner side thereby increasing the diameter of the tree each year and new inner bark

PLATE 52: **Dendrochronology**
Section through tree to expose growth rings

tissue towards its outer side. The exposed outer bark acts as a protective layer but comprises dead tissue.

A key fact in the dating process and cross matching is that although different trees will exhibit growth rings that differ in actual size for each year of growth the relative width will be the same, e.g. wide rings will show as wider rings in each tree for a particular year and similarly for narrow rings but actual growth widths will inevitably vary from tree to tree. This relates to climate and site detail. It is argued that the master time chronology built up from this scientific study and profiling of growth rings for particular areas and trees is unique and the long sequence of wide and narrow growth rings is unlikely to be repeated because year to year climatic variations are not identical. The reader is referred to Mr. C.W. Ferguson's paper as detailed in the bibliography for an exposition of this subject and the techniques and precision of sample testing involved. Tree ring measuring techniques include initial scanning and integrated microscope, and computer software and screen display and are calibrated to an accuracy of one-hundredth of a millimetre.

To conclude this section on the dating of timber-framed barns the reader will be aware that while the assistance of such scientific dating methods as dendrochronology and carbon 14 provide reliable data for specific timbers, subject to the careful selection and identification and preparation of core samples, recourse to historical records will also play an important role in a final determination of construction dates. Perhaps it rests eventually upon the "balance of probabilities".

CHAPTER **3**

The Kent Oasthouse

1. The Buildings : Roundels and Square Kilns Structure and Function

2. Hop Machinery and Equipment of the Period

3. Illustrations and Comment
    - The Former Whitbread Hop Farm at Beltring, Kent
    - Sissinghurst: The Barn and Oasthouse
    - Museum of Kent Life, Maidstone : Working Oasthouse and Hop Garden
    - Scotney Castle Estate: Little Scotney Farm and Westerham Brewery: Working Oast, Hop Garden and Brewery
    - Chartwell Oast, Spelmonden Oast at Goudhurst, Mote Farm Oast at Ightham,
    - Eden Farm Oast, West Malling, Kent
    - Hadlow Maltings Complex, Kent
    - Portmans Oast, Knockholt, Kent
    - Yonsea, Woodbridge, Kent
    - Goudhurst, Kent

PLATE 53: **Humulus Lupulus**
The Hop

3 The Kent Oasthouse

The whole purpose of the oasthouse is to dry hops to fit them for the brewing process. The use of the hop in brewing can be traced to the low countries of Europe in the 13th century and in England records indicate some imports of beer came from Flanders in the late 13th century and more so during the 14th century. By the end of the 15th century beer brewing in England is held to have been common in most towns and imports of hops were increasing. The transition was from the drinking of ale, comprising unhopped malted barley to beer which incorporated the resinous hop with its bitter flavour and preservative qualities which enabled the beer to continue in fresh condition sufficient to permit its transport from brewer around the town and between towns without detriment, thereby providing a stimulus for the growth of the brewing industry.

Mr. C. Dyer (Everyday Life in Medieval England) indicates that in the late 13th century a high proportion of women brewed quantities of ale for sale using either grain from their landholding or purchased malt for brewing, normally barley but in some areas oats were used. But at the end of the 14th century hops were in common use and instead of brewing a few hundred gallons of ale which had to be sold and consumed within a few days before it went sour, breweries could produce beer on a larger scale, store it and then convey it considerable distances to the relevant markets.

A further stimulus to the cultivation of hops was provided by population growth and the imposition of an import duty in 1690 of

20 shillings per hundredweight on foreign hops. A further duty of 28 shillings per hundredweight followed in 1710.

The term oasthouse refers to the complete building which comprises the kilns and the barn stowage into which the green hops are received and the dried hops stored ready for transport to the brewer or market. The sequence of activities flowed from the picking process in the hop gardens as the bines were cut from the hop poles strings or wires and stripped of their hops. The hops were heaped into the hop bins in the fields and subsequently weighed. Then followed the stowing of the green hops into pokes, being loosely woven sacks that helped the fresh hop to breathe and not sweat and deteriorate; then conveyance of the pokes each containing about 10 bushels was by horse drawn cart from the field to the oasthouse where the large sacks were hauled up by pulley to the upper floor ready to be emptied out and scuppetted onto the slatted floor of the drying kiln. Many hours later the dried hops were removed to a cooling floor and when ready, were compressed into large hop pockets (long sacks) originally by a man climbing into the suspended pocket and treading the hops. At a later date, about 1850, this process was performed by means of a hand operated rack and pinion mechanical compressing machine. The filled and compressed pockets were sewn tight and then stacked within the barn stowage area to await transport to the brewery for use. The pockets weighed about one and a half cwt.

The hop was grown on a commercial scale in England by the early sixteenth century and a very large number of oasthouses were constructed in Kent. Other areas important for hop cultivation were Sussex, Herefordshire, Hampshire, Worcestershire and Surrey but at the peak period of hop production in England Kent had some two thirds of the total acreage.

Hop Cultivation

Source : British Historical Statistics (B. R. Mitchell)

Year	Hop Acreage		
1867	64,000		
1876	70,000	)	
1878	72,000	)	The peak years of cultivation
1886	70,000		
1896	54,000		
1906	47,000		
1916	31,000	)	Probable consequence of WW1 impact on labour availability and a high excise duty on beer with reduced demand
1918	16,000	)	
1926	26,000		
1930	20,000	)	Acreage fairly constant throughout this
1966	20,000	)	period (lowest -17k highest 23k)
1980	14,000		Slow decline year on year from 20k in 1966

NB. In 2003 the national hop acreage had declined still further to some 3,000 acres of which only about 1,000 acres are in Kent.

Hop Production

Year	Thousands of Hundredweights	
1885	509	First year of records
1886	776	
1896	453	The years selected are to enable comparison between
1906	246	yields and acreage. Year on year the yields are shown to vary
1916	308	considerably/ The highest overall yield was in 1886 with
1918	130	776,000 hundredweight. 696,000 hundredweight are recorded in
1926	332	1905 when acreage had reduced to 49,000 acres.
1930	253	
1966	226	
1980	140	

NB. The import duty on foreign hops was removed in 1862. Increases in population increased the market potential for beer. By the end of the nineteenth century cheaper imported hops were reducing demand for English hops and acreages declined.

The Buildings

The earliest form of oasthouse was merely a small timber barn structure and conversion of existing farm outbuildings was not uncommon. The basic need was for an elevated slatted floor within the building under which some form of heating could be applied relying upon normal air convection to carry the warmth upward to dry the hops above. The need for an escape method (vent) for the heavy fumes given off by the drying process does not always seem to be satisfied since referrals to it are scarce but it is presumed an upper window in the barn may have served this purpose or perhaps some form of shutter or vent near the apex of the barn roof. Clearly ventilation would have been essential since the noxious fumes (the acid reek) given off in the drying process and any fumes from the heating source would have required a means of escape.

In 1574 Reynolde Scot published his book (A Perfite Platform of a Hoppe Garden) on the husbandry of the hop including the recommended design for an oasthouse. His small timber framed structure is depicted sectioned into three units, a green hop receiving area, a central drying kiln with honeycombed brick furnace, wood burning, and a third section for cooling the dried hops and bagging them for market. The stress was on the need for careful controlled hop drying to retain the quality of the hop resin.

The size of the building was to be some 19ft. long by 8ft.wide and was apparently suited for drying hops grown on about one acre of land. The drying floor was to be sited 5 ft. above the ground floor level. .No indication is given concerning the ventilation of the kiln but it was recommended that brick be used for the walls surrounding the furnace area to lessen the ever present risk of fire, particularly since the early structures had thatched roofs.

The scale of hop cultivation was very small in the 16th century and a norm per farm has been suggested as one acre. As hop production increased in the 17th to 19th century so the need for larger oasthouses also increased . The statistics for English hop cultivation set out above clearly demonstrate the trends in cultivation. The peak period for the English hop industry was the nineteenth century and it is to this period most of the existing oasthouses belong although varying in size, the square kiln or roundel designs are quite familiar sights and remain plentiful in Kent albeit mostly now converted to residential use. Contrary to the earlier style of inset kilns these new kilns were invariably built at one end of the barn stowage, sometimes at each end of the stowage or in larger structures the kilns were built along one elevation of the barn with intercommunicating doors to access the kiln area, drying floor and storage. etc.

The largest concentration of kilns is at the former Whitbread

Brewery Hop Garden at Beltring in Kent which has five large oasthouses and twenty-five kilns. A second concentration of kilns is found at Sissinghurst. Further comment on these two sites is included later.

The publication "Oasthouses in Sussex and Kent" by Gwen James and John Bell includes interesting details of two agreements for the construction of an oasthouse, the first is between a landowner and his tenant and two carpenters in 1667 for the building of an oasthouse at Flimwell in the parish of Ticehurst, East Sussex.

(i) The agreement provides for the landowner to provide sufficient rough timber (presumably from his own land) and the oasthouse is to measure 30ft. in length and 15ft. in width. The posts are to measure 10ft between the groundsill and wall plate. The two carpenters are to fell the timber where the landowner instructs and do all the carpentry work necessary for the building including making three doors, stairs and a partition between the chamber and oast. The agreement of the 6th August, 1667, stipulates all the work must be completed by the 20th November next. Payment (excluding timber) is three shillings a foot based upon the measurement of one wall along the building and one across. The tenant agreed to provide one rib of beef and 18 gallons (Kilderkin) of beer when the frame was reared.

(ii) The second agreement was made in February, 1671, when the same landowner commissioned another oasthouse but refers this time to two kilns. The timber structure was to measure thirty two feet in length and sixteen or seventeen feet in width with posts ten foot between groundsill and wall plate. Of particular note is that provision of an outlet vent is stipulated. The description of two kilns has been interpreted as referring to "one large kiln heated by two furnaces....in view of the fact only one vent was envisaged". This record is the first known occasion where a document specifies the forming of an outlet vent, the payment for the vent being at two pence the foot whereas for the oasthouse it is three shillings the foot for which the carpenters must fell the timber and make partitions, windows, stairs including boards for the chambers and for the kilns and all manner of carpenters' work necessary for the several uses of the building.

In the seventeenth century the timber framed ridge vented structures were increasingly roofed with clay tiles in preference to thatch, requiring therefore more substantial rafters to carry the weight but having the advantage of reduced fire risk. The need for draught control to help regulate temperature was evident with the inclusion of sliding shuttered windows that enabled relatively speedy changes to the level of air entering the kiln.

The square kiln measuring some 12ft. to 16ft. with pyramidal tiled roof became common in the late eighteenth century and brick construction although more expensive than timber frame was becoming the norm. The cowl with its fly board is thought to have been used in place of louvred roof vents from the mid 18th century. In the early nineteenth century a Mr. John Reade, a well known gardener of Horsmonden in Kent designed the first roundel kiln. Mr. J. Lake (Historic Farm Buildings) records the roundel as first appearing in Kent from 1815 and in Herefordshire by 1835. The plans of the roundel design were published in 1833 and the various advantages claimed for this form of kiln were that it prevented cold spots on the drying floor by the better distribution of heat. It was also said to be cheaper to construct than similar sized rectangular kiln and was stronger and more durable (claims later disputed).

In construction terms, the roundels were normally of two nine inch bricks (18ins or 14ins) to the eaves level upon which would be a timber wall plate. The rafters supported by the plate rise up to the timber, circular curb sited at the opening at the top of the conical roof. The cowl propelled by wind pressure on the fly board has a central spindle to permit it to revolve away from the prevailing wind, preventing entry of rain and wind to the oast and at the same time venting in the manner of a chimney fumes from the kiln beneath. The rafters are braced halfway to the top of the cone by a series of short horizontal timbers encircling the framework. The inside of the cone is lathed and plastered. The exterior is tiled to softwood battens. Tiles were of clay specially tapered to fit the cone roof. Tile covered oversailing brickwork at the eaves helped throw the rainwater clear of the roundel walls. The stowage area was often brick to first floor level then timber frame, weatherboarded and tarred or painted white. Stowage roofs being relatively small comprised rafters with tie-beam trusses and purlins for bracing. The king post features in the more recent buildings. Where local stone was readily available this was sometimes used instead of brick but walls were much thicker due to the random size of the stone. Stone roundels and stone rectangular kilns can be found at various sites in Kent.. The Museum of Kent Life near Maidstone is an example of such a stone oast, similarly the Kentish ragstone oast at Chartwell and again the ragstone roundels at Mote Farm, Ightham, Kent.

From the mid 19th century the roof of some roundels were built of brick using half bricks. They were plastered on the internal face and weatherproofed externally by a cement render often then covered with a bitumen protective layer. Roundels continued to be built in Kent and Sussex to the end of the nineteenth century and into early twentieth century.

Modern drying sheds are now huge steel framed and metal clad structures utilising automated mechanical aids and electric power, and oil fired heating, a far cry from the handsome relics of the rectangular pyramidal roofed kilns or conical roofed roundels of the earlier years that are the remains of an important part of our building heritage.

Machinery and Equipment

The oasthouse remained a relatively simple agricultural drying and storage barn up until the late nineteenth century being the period with which this specific commentary is primarily concerned. The equipment to be considered is the roof cowl and its function, the heating apparatus for drying the green hops and the nature of the drying floor particularly how it allowed warm air to permeate to the hops. The machinery included the mechanical press to compress the dried/cooled hops into the long pockets, fans that either pulled up the moist air and fumes from the kiln or alternatively provided a controlled draft of air from below to accelerate the drying process.

Other minor equipment found in the oasthouse is the simple pulley to raise or lower the heavy sacks of hops to and from the first floor level of the stowage barn. The long hop pockets (jute sacks about six foot tall) of compressed hops each weigh about 180 lbs. Metal hand held hooks were used to assist the handlers in moving the large awkward pokes and pockets around. Also low four wheeled barrows were useful to convey the pockets to the stowage area and subsequently outside to be hoisted onto the cart for transport to the brewery. Wide toothed wooden rakes were used to level the green hops as they were spread onto the kiln drying floor and an implement called a scuppet to shovel the green hops into the kiln and subsequently out of the kiln to the cooling floor and then into the hop pockets for compressing. Lighting within the oasthouse was poor as there were limited windows. In the earliest days they would have used candles inserted within a lantern case to lessen the fire risk; then from the late nineteenth century paraffin lamps and in more recent times hurricane lamps, etc. until electricity became available.

The Cowl

The cowl appears to have been introduced in the mid eighteenth century to replace the louvred ridge vents. Constructed of wood the cowl is a part enclosed near cone shaped apparatus some ten foot tall and open for about one third of its circumference the opening being the vent through which the warm air and acrid fumes are expelled from the rectangular or roundel kiln. A central spindle (post) framed into the cowl descends vertically down through the opening in the kiln roof and the whole weight of the cowl is supported by means of this spindle on two horizontal stout beams set at rightangles to each other and secured either into the brickwork of the kiln roof or morticed and tenoned into the principal rafters of a timber and plastered cone shaped or pyramidal roof. The spindle has a metal end resting freely within a metal cup fixed to the upper surface of the supporting beams and this enables the spindle and cowl to revolve when wind pressure on the extended horizontal fly board, acted like a weather vane, to turn the closed face of the cowl towards the prevailing wind. The spindle is supported at its upper end as it passes through the wooden curb located at the top of the kiln roof by a metal collar itself fastened to the curb. This permits free rotation of the spindle within the collar.

Drying Floor And Heating Source

The recommended drying floor had, at least from Reynolde Scot's time (book published 1574) been one situated above a heating source or type of furnace and comprising timber joists upon which a floor of wooden slats was set closely together to permit warm air to penetrate and dry the hops above but not wide enough so that the hops could fall through the gaps onto the fires below. Later the trend was for the slatted floor to be covered over with a coarsely woven horsehair mat onto which the green hops were spread. Dependent upon how moist the fresh hops were they could be spread to a depth of eight inches or so. As drying efficiencies improved a depth of twice this could be achieved. Early forms of heating included types of fixed open grate or removable brazier upon which wood was burned. Materials which would flare or spark were omitted. Later, fuels included charcoal or anthracite. The problem was to try to prevent gases from the fire from contaminating the hops above and to maintain an even temperature without cold spots.

In Scot's book the recommended furnace was one constructed of brick with a honeycombed side panel that allowed heat and fumes to disperse around the heating chamber. Bricks tilted on end and cemented along the top of the fire chamber enclosed it therefore reducing spark emissions. In the mid to late eighteenth century a system of enclosed stove heating became more common with warm air ducted via a system of metal flue pipes all around the plenum chamber directly beneath the drying floor and by this method trying to ensure all potential cold spots were eliminated. The flue pipe vented the fire's fumes through the kiln's external wall therefore avoiding hop contamination.

The Use of Fans

Normal process of drying depended upon convection with warm air rising from the heat source up through the drying floor and out through the roof vent or cowl. Time is money, and it was inevitably the driving force for the introduction of fanned ventilation since this method generated a greater volume of air and permitted deeper beds of green hops to be dried more quickly than with normal convection. Two forms of fan were commonly in use. The first were those set at the base of the kiln housed within a brick ducting on an outside wall. They blew large controlled volumes of air into the lower kiln. The second type of fan was one set high up on the outside of the kiln in a framed housing and operated by pulling air up from within the kiln. Prior to electricity the fans were mechanically driven by belt power linked to a steam engine or tractor.

The Mechanical Hop Press

The jute pockets are suspended from a round hole cut into the floorboards of the cooling floor on the first floor of the oasthouse. Dried and cooled hops were manually scuppetted into the sacks. As the sack filled it was necessary for someone to climb into the suspended pocket to tread the hops down and a succession of filling and treading followed until the pocket was full and it could be sewn closed. To help support the pocket throughout this process in addition to being fastened at its upper end to a frame surrounding the hole, a belt or rope was looped underneath the pocket to help take the weight. The treading process was clearly a chokingly dirty labour with the operative smothered in the hop resin. About 1850 the mechanical hop press came into use comprising a heavy timber frame with cast iron rack and pinion mechanism operated by a large wheel shaped handle that could lower a heavy circular metal disc down through the hole cut in the cooling floor and thereby compressed the dried hops in the pocket. This enabled the bagging process to be completed much more quickly than by the manual treading process.

PLATE 54 Beltring Hop Farm
Oasthouse with five external circular kilns and puller fans (Bell Field)

Former Whitbread Hop Farm Beltring, Kent

For over four hundred years farms in the Yalding area of Kent had been cultivating the hop, but it was in 1920 that the Whitbread brewing company purchased farmland at Beltring subsequently adding to its land holding until records indicate it had over 300 acres of hops in cultivation. Four principal oasthouses each having five brick roundels (kilns) and Kent clay pegged tile roofs are situated on the Bell field at Beltring and are dated to the 1880's. A fifth oast with five internal kilns and cowls positioned along the stowage ridge was built in 1936. The stowage was constructed of brick with steel roof trusses.

A large temporary labour force recruited from London was essential in September of each year to pick the green hops. The twenty kilns (1880's) were each loaded with some fifty pokes of hops twice in each twenty four hour period. The drying process was continuous night and day until all the hops were processed. Since a poke contained about ten bushels of hops fifty pokes represented five hundred bushels for each kiln load and twenty kilns therefore could process ten thousand bushels for each drying period. With two drying periods in each twenty-four hours a throughput of twenty thousand bushels could be achieved.

PLATE 55: **Beltring Hop Farm**
two oasthouses in line on Bell Field (External kilns) (1880)

PLATE 56: **Beltring Hop Farm**
Oasthouse with five internal kilns venting through the roof.

Oast Construction

Mr. R. Walton in his "History of Beltring Hop Farm" sets out detailed and informative background to the farm, the various oasthouses and their key features including data for oasts no longer in existence. Much of the Beltring information is taken from the on site hop exhibition and that record.

The four principal oasthouses (1880) remaining in Bell Field each have five twenty foot diameter brick roundels set along a brick, side elevation, of each separate stowage. The stowage of Bell oasts one and two is twenty-six feet wide by one hundred feet long. Bell oasts three and four are twenty-nine feet wide and one hundred and ten feet long. The latter comprise three storeys and the former two storeys. All four oast stowages are built of brick on three sides with timber framed front elevations covered with wooden boarding and painted white. The kiln drying floors are of open timber slats covered with horsehair matting. The roofs are covered with hand-made clay pegged tiles. Plates 54 and 55 illustrate these oasthouses including the brick kilns with their puller fan systems and the external metal flues that discharge the coke or oil fired boiler fumes. Three of the five oasthouses were in use for hop drying into the 1980's but drying finally finished in these kilns in 1984.

Whitbread sold the farm in 1992 and the whole complex is now used as hop farm country park with a museum of hop farming, shire horse displays and an activity centre. Many of the buildings are Grade II listed

PLATE 57: **Sissinghurst Castle Barn**
Elizabethan Barn : Front elevation.. depicts wagon door, ventilation slits and buttressing.

Sissinghurst Castle Estate, Kent

The estate of Sissinghurst Castle notable for the Vita Sackville-West gardens and now under National Trust ownership and management also contains important farm buildings. An Elizabethan brick barn is sited within a complex of agricultural buildings that include a granary (converted to restaurant), a single storey weatherboard barn (used as the Trust souvenir shop) and an imposing oasthouse comprising six square kilns and two large roundels. Within the oasthouse is an exhibition that includes a wooden hop press, hop pocket and a slatted and horsehair covered hop drying floor.

The box frame brick barn built in the second half of the 16th century has a single centrally sited wagon door but no porch. On the opposite side is a similarly large doorway with a raised loading bay made possible due to the land sloping sharply away on that side. The barn has six brick buttresses on each side and the brickwork is in English bond. Ventilation is by a series of narrow brick vents in the side elevations. The barn roof is fully supported by the brick walls. There are no vertical posts to assist with carrying the load to the ground. Five substantial tie beams are set across the barn and each has queen posts sited centrally rising to a collar beam A further two heavy transverse beams are set into the brick wall just below the wall plate at one end of the barn The roof covering is of clay peg tiles to battens.

The six square oast kilns are thought to have been constructed in the 18th century. They are twelve feet square and were originally coal fired. In the 19th century two eighteen foot diameter brick roundels were added to the structure. These latter had fans built into a duct of honeycombed brickwork at the base of the outer wall of each roundel to increase the draft forced up through the kiln to improve hop drying efficiency. The cowls are the vents that enable the acrid reek from the drying hops to be discharged from the kiln and by rotating with the wind the cowls shield the kiln from rain and downdraught. The name of the fan manufactures is visible on the metal framing of the fan units (blades now absent) and is James Keith Blackman. The brickwork of the kilns is of interest, the two roundels being in English Bond and the six square kilns on one elevation are Flemish bond with two brick buttresses while on the opposite flank there are four brick buttresses and brickwork is in English Garden Wall Bond comprising three stretcher courses to one header course.

Particulars of farm activities at Sissinghurst estate indicate the kilns have not been used for hop drying since 1967. The farm is still worked by Messrs. Beales and Stearns and comprises 232 acres of licensed land and 140 acres of woodland. Until 1960 it grew hops, fruit and arable crops and had a dairy herd of 40 cows. Today, the crops are mainly wheat, barley and oil seed rape. The pastures were grazed by sheep and beef cattle but these have long since gone. More recently the National Trust has begun exploring the practicality of using some of the farmland to grow produce to use in the Granary Restaurant

PLATE 58: **Sissinghurst Castle Barn**
Roof trusses with Queen posts

PLATE 59: Sissinghurst Castle Oast
Side elevation showing the six square kilns

PLATE 60: **Sissinghurst Castle Oast**
Opposite side showing the two roundels

PLATE 61: **Sissinghurst Castle Oast**
Close-up of fan ventilation units at base of roundels

PLATE 62: **Sissinghurst Castle Oast**
Rack and Pinion Hop Press

PLATE 63: **Sissinghurst Castle Oast**
Kiln Drying Floor - Slatted

PLATE 64: **Sissinghurst Castle Oast**
Beam Supports for Cowl Spindle within Cone Roof of Roundel

Cobtree: Museum of Kent Life, Maidstone

The Museum of Kent Life was established by Kent County Council and Maidstone Borough Council in 1984 at the former Sandling farm, Cobtree Manor, Maidstone. The 28 acre complex includes a coal-fired working oasthouse and a small hop garden, a number of hoppers' huts, a timber frame and thatched barn, granary and other buildings. The nineteenth century oasthouse was derelict and fire damaged but restoration work has included rebuilding of one square eighteen foot kiln, two sixteen foot diameter roundels and the stowage. The oasthouse is built of Kentish ragstone.

PLATE 65a: **Sandling Farm**
Museum of Kent Life : Oasthouse (Ragstone Roundels and Square Kiln)

PLATE 65b: **Sandling Farm**
Museum of Kent Life : Oasthouse (Ragstone Roundels and Square Kiln)

PLATE 65c: **Sandling Farm Barn**
Timber framed and weatherboarded

PLATE 65d: **Sandling Farm Barn**
Single hipped canopy cart entrance

PLATE 65e: **Sandling Farm Barn**
Internal view of aisled barn

PLATE 66: **Sandling Farm**
Museum of Kent Life : Hop Pocket

PLATE 67: **Sandling Farm**
Illustrates a four-wheeled barrow for conveying hop pockets and for muck spreading

PLATE 68: **Scotney Castle Estate** *illustrates the timber framed barn with tile roof*

Little Scotney Farm and Westerham Brewery Company

Within the Scotney Castle gardens estate lies Little Scotney farm which amongst other crops cultivates the hop. The farm has a nucleated complex of buildings including house, oasthouse with four brick roundels and a separate modern barn. In the lower fields the traditional hop garden is at its best by September when picking of the green hops begins with the help of a temporary labour force. Scotney is the only hop farm owned by the National Trust and is run by its tenant farmer. The Trust also entered into a joint project with the tenant farmer of its Crockham Grange Farm at Crockham Hill near Westerham and facilitated the development of a new brewing business in 2004 by providing and allowing the owner and manager of the brewery to adapt the old dairy building which involved new concrete floors and stainless steel drainage. The brewery uses hops grown by Little Scotney farm (Wye Target Hops).

Within the Scotney Castle estate but separate from the farm complex is a timber framed barn. The roof is Queen Post and covered with clay tiles, the barn walls are unclad but the structure is generally sound. There are no aisles.

PLATE 69: **Scotney Castle Estate**
Queen Post tie beams, posts and bracing. The Queen posts are lapped to the collar beams into which the purlins are notched.

PLATE 696: **Little Scotney Farm**
Oasthouse with four roundels

PLATE 69c: **Little Scotney Farm**
Hop gardens

The Kent Oasthouse | 187

Chartwell, Kent

PLATE 70a: **Chartwell**
Illustrates the Kentish ragstone oasthouse with three roundels. The building has been converted to residential use. A second two roundel oast is also shown.

PLATE 70b: **Chartwell**

Illustrates the Kentish ragstone oasthouse with three roundels. The building has been converted to residential use. A second two roundel oast is also shown.

Spelmonden Oast, Goudhurst, Kent

Plate 71 illustrates the brick oasthouse comprising five roundels and stowage. The building has been well converted to commercial office use. Brickwork is evidently recent and in English bond with dog tooth decoration at the eaves. The roof is Kent clay tile. The flyboards on the cowls depict Invicta, the rearing horse of Kent.

PLATE 71: Spelmonden

Mote Farm, Ightham, Kent

Sited across a narrow lane from Ightham Mote the farm buildings are extensive and a mix of styles including modern barns. The oasthouse is constructed of Kentish ragstone and includes four roundel kilns with clay tile roofs.

PLATE 72a: **Mote Farm, Ightham**

PLATE 72b: Mote Farm, Ightham

PLATE 72c: **Mote Farm**
Ragstone Barn with half-hipped clay tiled roof

West Malling : Oasthouse At Eden Farm, Kent

The oast complex comprises four twenty foot diameter brick roundels constructed at one end of a substantial two storey brick stowage barn. Roofs are of Kent clay peg tile. At the time of my visit to the site in 1986 the buildings were at an advanced stage of conversion to residential use. The principal part of the stowage barn had already been separated by internal brick walling from the roundels and was in occupation. The four large kilns and remaining part of the barn were in the process of conversion into two further residential units of approximately equal size. Foul sewer drainage pipework had been laid to connect to the main sewer at the junction with the highway. Roundel brickwork is in Flemish bond with dogtooth decorative at the eaves. The walls are 13 ½ inches thick to the first floor level and 9 inches to the eaves. Kentish ragstone formed the original foundations for the kilns. Outcrops of the ragstone appear at several places in the surrounding fields.

PLATE 73: Eden Farm, West Malling
Brick Oasthouse (Residential Conversion)

The Kent Oasthouse

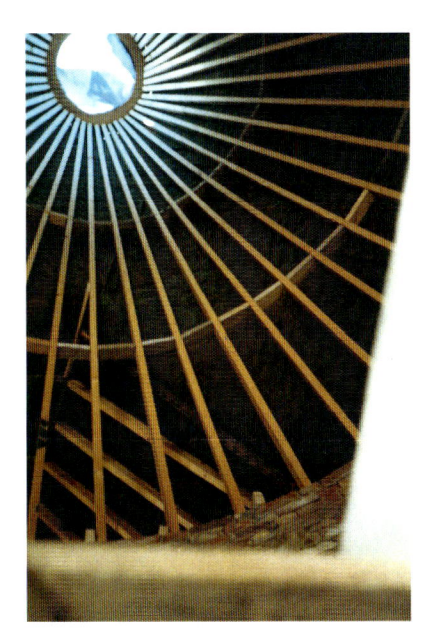

PLATE 74: **Eden Farm, West Malling**
Illustrates the reconstruction carpentry within the kiln's cone-shaped roof

PLATE 75: **Eden Farm, West Malling**
illustrates the ragstone foundation.

Hadlow Maltings, Kent

Plate 76 illustrates the four large square brick kilns with slate roofs of the former maltings at Hadlow which was converted to residential units in 1997.

PLATE 76: **Hadlow Maltings**
Residential Conversion

Portmans Oast, Knockholt, Kent

The single roundel oast and stowage has long been converted to residential use. The building is of knapped flint with brick banding.

PLATE 77: **Portman's Oast, Knockholt**
Illustrates the oasthouse

Yonsea Farm, Woodchurch, Kent

Plate 78 illustrates the brick oasthouse with two brick kilns and slate roof. The kilns are of eighteen inch brick in header bond up to the drying floor level and then fourteen inch brick in Flemish bond to the eaves. At the time of my visit in 2006 the cowls were absent. The Georgian Yonsea Farm buildings have been relocated from their original site by the Traditional Buildings Preservation Trust because it was established they were in danger of being lost due to the Channel Tunnel railway development. The Trust is re-erecting the farm buildings as funding becomes available. In addition to the oasthouse, a granary has been rebuilt. The timber framed barn was dismantled and transported to Woodchurch where it is in store awaiting re-erection.

PLATE 78: Yonsea Farm, Woodchurch

Oasthouse

PLATE 79: **Yonsea Farm, Woodchurch**
Granary with cart shed

Goudhurst, Kent

Situated in the heart of the Kent Hop country is this splendid example of a square kiln brick oasthouse with its white painted weatherboard and red clay tiled roof.

PLATE 80: **Goudhurst**
Square kiln oasthouse - residential conversion

CHAPTER **4**

Barns and Oasthouses Brickwork and Decorative Features

A. Types Of Brick Bond

B. Decorative Features

Dentillation

Dogtooth

Diaper

Brick Noggin

4   Brickwork And Decorative Features : Barns And Oasts

As a measure of completeness a short summary of aspects of the use of brick in early English barns and the much later oast buildings including the associated decorative features is considered. In medieval times it was common for bricks to be made from local clays found near to the site where building work was to take place. Skilled brickmakers, many of whom came from the continent, were essential to select the clay manage the building of clamps and to control the firing process. The fuel was wood or charcoal and the firing process could last days dependent upon the size of the clamp. Local labour would undertake the heavy work of digging the clay by hand, extracting the stones and preparing clay for use by the brickmakers. The skilled workers were necessarily nomadic and moved from site to site to seek new work.

    The economics of the brick making process were characterised by a low value and heavy product difficult and expensive to convey large distances especially when river carriage was not practical. Pack horse or horse and cart were the main means of transport with poor roads and track ways. This meant the cost of bricks at the building site would be considerably higher than the cost at the brickfield. The need to source site specific clays was therefore a major influence on building with brick.

    As transport facilities improved bulk transport of bricks became economic using metalled roads and the canal system. The brick industry rapidly developed and large scale brickfields became the norm having the benefit scale brings and with improved kilns and mechanical brick production meant labour requirements were reduced and corresponding expense. Cartage costs remain however a significant element of brick supply.

There are many early examples of brick built barns. The full weight of the roof timbers and tiles falls directly onto the brick walls which have to be strong enough to resist the crushing forces. As with stone barns, the use of buttresses is common to counteract the enormous pressures exerted by the downward and outward thrust of the barn roof. In timber frame barns, bricks were often used to form a plinth or low wall onto which the substantial groundsill timbers could be placed to carry the great structural timbers of a post and truss barn. The brick plinth would provide a degree of protection to the timbers elevating the sill above the soil to prevent the drawing up of ground moisture and consequent rotting.

Oasthouse roundels or square kilns were invariably constructed of brick or stone, the associated storage barn similarly but in the earliest oasts they would be of timber frame with weatherboard cladding.

Bricks come in a wide range of colours and shapes. Brick clay comprises a mixture of sand and alumina and contains a variety of trace elements dependent upon where it is found e.g. lime, chalk, iron oxide, manganese dioxide, etc. and these elements influence the colour of the brick when fired, although the nature of the firing process and temperature and position in the clamp or kiln also affects colour.

In medieval times the clay when prepared was moulded by hand using sanded wooden moulds the process being clearly demonstrated in the illuminated manuscripts and stained glass depictions of that time. The moulded clay blocks were carefully stacked on pallets for drying and when ready the blocks were fired in a clamp or kiln to produce a hard brick with protective fireskin ready for building. Today, mechanical processes produce bricks by the wire cut extruded method e.g. perforated bricks, or machine moulded by hydraulic press. The brick kilns at the permanent brick fields fire many thousands of bricks at each firing. Some hand made bricks are still made for special uses including conservation and restoration work on listed buildings. Another form of brick made today is the concrete brick comprising crushed rock aggregate with portland cement and dyed with a pigment.

Type of Bricks and Bonds

Facing bricks are for exposed surfaces where appearance , texture, colour and unblemished consistency are important. A fletton or stock brick is for more general use. Engineering bricks, mostly blue-grey in colour are very hard and with low absorption of water being often used in civil engineering works. Elsewhere they are used in capping of walls or in decorative features in a wall, either as banding or in lintel effects over windows and doors where bricks are stood vertically on end with the stretcher face showing. Bricks displayed in this latter fashion are termed soldiers. Bricks varied in size in medieval times often thinner than those of today. "Great brickes" were 12 inches long, 6 inches wide and 3 inches thick. At Beverley (1550) bricks of 10 ½ inches by 5 ¼ inches by 2 inches thick were made. They were standardised in the Brickmakers Charter (1571) at 9ins. x 4 1/2 ins. x 2 1/4ins. However sizes continued to fluctuate.

A stretcher is the longer face of a brick normally showing horizontally in the courses of a wall. A header is the end face of a standard brick. A bat is part of a brick e.g. half or three-quarters and is used in bond work to achieve the staggered effect. For purposes of strength and in order to distribute the compression load bricks are laid in a bond that ensures vertical joints are staggered or offset (alignment is visually important). The bed joint (horizontal joint) of one course of bricks laid on another course is unaffected. Types of bond or arrangement of bricks are illustrated below.

1. **The English Bond** (Plate 81)
   This comprises alternate courses of headers and stretchers. Note the offset or overlap effect to stagger the vertical jointing. English Bond was the generally used form of brickwork in the late medieval period up to the early part of the 17th century when it was replaced in favour of Flemish bond. In the earlier years it seems irregular use of brick bonding was not exceptional. The bonding format being intermittent and haphazard.

   The two roundels in the oasthouse at Sissinghurst demonstrate English Bond, similarly the roundels at Spelmondon.

PLATE 81: **Brickwork**
English Bond

PLATE 82: **Brickwork**
Flemish Bond

2. **Flemish Bond** (Plate 82)
    This uses headers and stretchers side by side in each course of bricks. The oast houses at Beltring and West Malling demonstrate Flemish bond but note the irregularity where the brickwork has been cut to provide for the window in conversion. A variation in this method was the Flemish stretcher bond which used header and stretcher side by side on one course followed by a stretcher course.

3. **English Garden Wall Bond** (Plate 83)
    Three/five courses of stretchers to one course of headers. The square kilns at Sissinghurst are constructed in English Garden Wall Bond on one elevation.

4. **Header Bond** (Plate 84)
    Bricks used with header of the brick showing. Note the partial over lap in vertical joints. Particularly useful in curved walls. The lower section from foundation to drying floor level of the oasthouse at Yonsea Farm demonstrates header bond.

PLATE 83: **Brickwork**
English Garden Wall Bond

210 | The Early English Barn & The Kent Oasthouse

PLATE 84: **Brickwork**
Header Bond

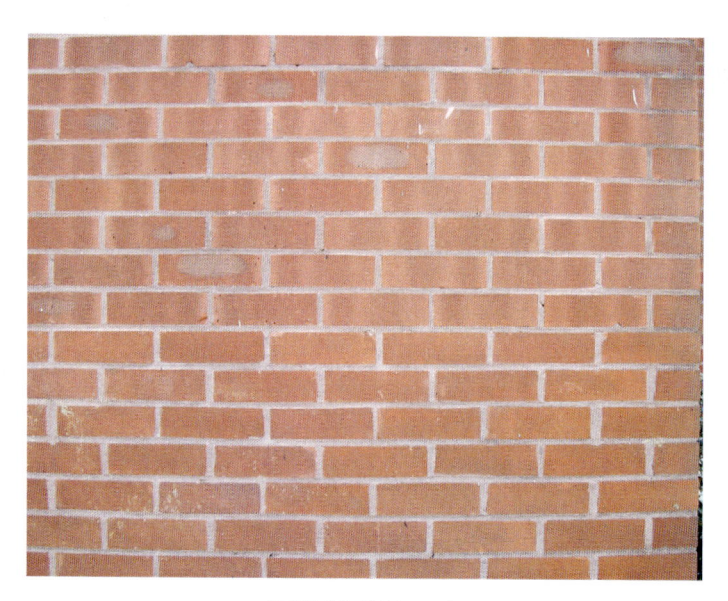

PLATE 85: **Brickwork**
Stretcher Bond

5. **Stretcher Bond** (Plate 85)
    Bricks laid horizontally with stretcher face showing the staggering of row upon row being achieved by using cut bricks (BAT) at the end of or even within the row. This is a very commonly used bond in building today.

Decorative Brickwork

Decorative features are introduced by the use of different coloured bricks or by using projecting or recessed bricks and sometimes with special shaped bricks. Specific features are the diaper effect (diagonal intersections or diamond shapes), dentil or dog tooth, variations of basket weave and herringbone and brick banding features. An example of dog tooth brickwork (a row of bricks set at 45 degrees to the wall face) is well illustrated on the oast roundel at West Malling, Kent. (Plate 86). Another example is the oast house complex at Spelmondon (Plate 87). Note the protruding brick banding above and below the dog tooth. The dentil effect is created by a regular pattern of projecting headers and is found in the roundels at Beltring. (Plate 88). Here again we see a banding of protruding stretchers above and below the dentil headers.

A fine example of brick banding is found at the Portmans Oast at Knockholt in Kent Note the knapped flint of the walls and the distinctive decorative bands of brick both in the horizontal and the vertical. The brickwork adds to the strength of the lime mortared flint.

An example of diaper brickwork is seen at the 16th century Tudor building called Shurland House on the Isle of Sheppey . This Grade II star property is currently under restoration financed by a grant of £300,000 from English Heritage. The restoration work is under the direction of the Spitalfields Trust and includes for the relocation of two large grain silos from the nearby farm buildings (Plate 90).

The gable and front elevation of the 16th century brick barn at Copdock near Ipswich also displays the diamond pattern. A further example is the boundary wall at Chapel barn, Place Farm, Chiddingly in East Sussex. The barn commenced life in circa 1500 as an Elizabethan manor house and was partly converted to a barn in circa 1600. In the late 20th century it has been re-converted to residential use (Plate 89).

PLATE 86: **Decorative Features**
Dog Tooth at Eaves - West Malling

PLATE 87: **Decorative Features**
Dog Tooth at Eaves - Spelmonden

PLATE 88: **Decorative Features**
Dentil at Eaves - Beltring

PLATE 89: **Decorative Features**
Diaper Pattern - Chapel Barn, Chiddingly

Crow stepped gable decoration is evident at Hales brick barn (15th century) in Norfolk and at Copdock, the latter having massive brick buttresses. Various plates earlier in this book illustrate the use of the brick plinth in timber framed barn structures.

At Cressing Temple the Wheatbarn had its wall planking replaced in the sixteenth century by brick noggin infill panels (Plate 91).

PLATE 90: **Decorative Features**
Diaper Pattern - Shurland House

PLATE 91: Decorative Features

Brick Noggin between close studding at Cressing Temple wheat barn

Efflorescence

It is not uncommon to see brick walls displaying a white powdery deposit over the face of the brickwork. This is probably the result of the drying or crystallization of soluble salts discharged from the bricks following a period of heavy wetting. In contrast lime staining (insoluble calcarious deposits) also discolours the brickwork but is from the portland cement contained within the mortar or concrete. An example of lime staining is shown at Plate 92 in which the staining can be clearly seen to emanate from the cement mortar jointing.

PLATE 92: **Brickwork**
Lime Staining

CHAPTER **5**

Barns and Oasts Planning and Legal Issues

(i) The Problem of Redundant Barn Structures Conservation, Adaptive Re-Use, Conversion

(ii) Planning Constraints, Legal Considerations and Law Cases

5 Barns and Oasthouses

The Problem Of Redundant Barn Structures

Early English barns, listed or otherwise, are distinctive and vast agricultural features in the landscape. They represent a valuable cultural legacy, are historically important and present examples of highly developed crafts and skills. They demand and deserve conservation.

Reality in farming terms presents a quite different picture. Nineteenth and twentieth century mechanisation of agriculture, changes and diversification in patterns of farm management with mergers into larger more viable units have all impacted adversely upon the continuing usefulness of old barns. Farm incomes have recorded a dramatic decline since the 1990's many farms have gone out of business or become "hobby" farms of the otherwise wealthy . Inheritance tax advantage by means of agricultural property relief adds to this. Other farms are broken up.

A high proportion of listed farm buildings are in an advance state of structural decay. The tithe barns and other early barns may no longer serve a useful purpose for the farmer being of limited access via the cart doors and internal space is hindered by the arcade posts which preclude sheltering of the huge combine harvesters and tractors commonly in use today. The farmer can ill afford to carry the burden of financing the heavy maintenance cost of a large structure that offers him little practical use. What then is the answer? The problem has challenged the many public bodies concerned with the protection of the rural environment and recommended options for the use of redundant farm buildings as opposed to demolition or allowing them to further decay now seek to encourage a more diversified approach. If conservation of that which exists is impractical then adapting the building for some other beneficial use whilst retaining the integrity of the original structure and its appearance in the countryside is the preferred option. Clearly any change in use of a farm building particularly a listed barn will require local authority planning consent including listed buildings consent. Preservation of the countryside is a prime responsibility of the planning control mechanisms therefore proposals for alternative use of barns will need to be carefully focused and surmount the many controls that operate to prevent unsuitable rural development. Early consultation with the local conservation officer and planning department seeking their views and guidance is the proven approach to possible consent.

From the farmer's standpoint if he has no use for his listed barn for agricultural purposes or even for storage it is possible to consider adaptive re-use for letting as small workshop units to encourage local crafts or trades, the rents from the lettings yielding a welcome addition to depleted farm incomes and providing local employment. Some farmers have converted barns into residential units for holiday lets thereby creating a secondary income source. In other cases the structures have successfully converted for use as offices thereby generating rental income. Farm shops present a further option.

The sheer size of the barns with their huge internal usable space is considered to make them suitable for community activities and conversions for this purpose have in some cases proved successful but in practical terms barns can be draughty halls, difficult to heat. Expensively generated warm air rises to be lost in the cavernous roof spaces as well as escaping through the poorly insulated walls. When recently discussing with the trust managing a timber framed 13th century barn in Kent it was indicated that a letting had been made for a wedding reception but inclement weather with high winds had made the barn so cold and creaky during the evening it had nearly led to abandonment part way through. They feel it imprudent to venture again.

When the farmer prefers to dispose of a redundant barn in order to take immediate advantage of a large capital receipt and strengthen his finances or for re-investment in further land the onus for permitted conversion consent will rest with the purchaser. Prior consultation with the local planners as to possibilities would be prudent.

Many fine agricultural buildings and barns, some considered to be the finest of their type have been preserved for posterity through the direct action of English Heritage and the National Trust. The barns are being restored by means of grants from the Heritage Lottery Fund and money raised by national and local appeals. In other cases local preservation trusts have taken the initiative and with grant aid and a range of other fund raising initiatives have successfully secured and repaired specific farm buildings and barns of merit. In each of these cases the buildings are opened to the public and normally will be made available for general community use, meetings, lectures and social events of many kinds. They are invariably not self-financing and require considerable input from voluntary helpers to manage the property and rely on grants and continuous fund raising to sustain the fabric. It is reassuring to know that voluntary help on this large scale continues to be forthcoming.

The work of the Society for the Protection of Ancient Buildings (SPAB) over many years has had considerable and positive effect on the protection and preservation of historically important buildings through its role in vetting and advising on proposed planning applications affecting all manner of old buildings including churches, town houses, manor houses and farm property, barns, mills, etc. and whilst preferring and emphasising conservation with conservative repair, where lack of use is evidenced and continuing decay of buildings is inevitable, its approach favours the least intrusive form of conversion that retains as much as possible of the original fabric, its character and style. The best conversions are those that retain the barn's essential characteristics, size, enormous internal space, huge, often wavy, roof and old materials such as peg tiles or thatch, weatherboard cladding or stone or flint walls. Lack of windows is a particular problem. The SPAB readily offers advice to guide and assist potential conversions but will quite properly seek to deter and resist unsympathetic schemes.

When considering conversion of barns for residential occupation, considered the least desirable option and yet statistically the most usual conversion, a barn set within a village or at its boundary (the planning envelope concept) is more likely to receive planning consent than an isolated field barn which could be challenged as intrusive development in open countryside. In terms of finance, the availability of essential supply services such as electricity, water, sewerage, telephone is more likely in a village setting, and consequently less costly to connect the supplies than for the isolated barn. In the latter case the need for an access road across fields to reach the barn, garages for cars and hard standing, garden area, etc. is all intrusive in what is currently open land. The planning constraints in such a situation will be difficult to satisfy.

Planning Constraints, Legal Considerations and Law Cases

A very early priority in the process of barn conversions or the conversion of agricultural buildings generally e.g. stable, cowsheds, oasts, granaries, etc., is the need to clarify the specific planning constraints and the regional and local development plans for the area concerned. Liaison with the local planning authority becomes a pre-requisite and familiarity with planning law desirable.

1990 Planning Act : it is a criminal offence to demolish or to carry out works to a listed building without the prior consent from the local planning authority and other relevant authorities. On purchasing a listed building it is also crucial to check that any works already undertaken to the structure have been properly authorised. Unauthorised works will not only complicate and delay the acquisition but probably result in the planning authority requiring potentially expensive works to be undertaken to redress the transgression.

1990 Listed Building Act (Section 88) : Empowers conservation officers to inspect listed buildings to determine whether any illegal work has been carried out. The owner may not refuse access. The Conservation Officer has a dominant role in the matter of proposed works to listed buildings and operates within a framework of guidelines issued by English Heritage and the Department of Culture, Media and Sport. Listed buildings are those buildings legally recorded on a national register as properties of architectural or historic interest in terms of their style and character. Owners have a duty to ensure such buildings are properly maintained since they represent a legacy of national importance. Listing is currently structured in a hierarchy of Grade I (the highest), Grade II star, Grade II, but at the time of writing these are under review and the understanding is that some relaxation in the grading will be introduced. Local authorities may also maintain their own subordinate lists of buildings of local merit.

Other matters with which the potential converter of barns should become familiar are :

Government Policy Guidelines : in particular Planning Policy Guideline 7 "The Countryside, Environmental Quality and Economic and Social Development. It will be of little comfort to note government considers "Residential conversions are often detrimental to the character of historic farm buildings". Changes to the planning control regime are under consideration at the time of writing and indications are that some relaxation in the stringent controls will be permitted. This itself could result in further controversy.

National Farmers' Union : where there is no money or motive to restore buildings for agricultural purposes it would support other uses.

Royal Town Planning Institute : Farm buildings in village streets might work as houses but generally not those in rural locations. They comment that barns are often in isolated places and when converted into a dwelling introduce all the paraphernalia of domestic life into the open landscape and this is intrusive.

Council for the Protection of Rural England : Redundant barns of no architectural interest should be demolished. They are concerned that if converted to dwellings there will be a tendency over time for the original restrictions imposed on the conversion to be eroded in an incremental manner as the owners come to face the realities of domestic life in a converted barn.

English Heritage : Two recent publications set out matters of crucial importance to anyone considering the future use of traditional farm buildings.

(i) Living Buildings in a Living Landscape : (finding a future for traditional farm buildings). This document was produced jointly by English Heritage, The Countryside Agency's Landscape, Access and Recreation division and the University of Gloucestershire's Countryside and Community Research Unit. Potential converters of farm buildings will find the background information contained in this document of considerable help in setting the scene for adaptive re-use of farm buildings including comments on residential conversion.

(ii) The second publication : The Conversion of Traditional Farm Buildings : A Guide to Good Practice. This provides quite detailed guidance on the adapting and repair of traditional farm buildings, in particular the treatment of external walling, roofing, internal spaces, services and insulation, windows and doors, rainwater goods.

One final challenge facing the would be converter are building regulations and the health and safety requirements that will inevitably impact upon the proposed conversion which by its nature will be a material change of use. Close liaison with the relevant authorities is clearly essential at a very early stage since lack of compliance may demand an expensive corrective consequence.

Building Regulations

The technical requirements of Schedule 1 of the Building Regulations are grouped into thirteen parts and the broad categories are as follows: at the time of writing (October, 2006) they are under review.

1. Property Structure : loading, ground movement, wall thickness, timber sizes, etc.

2. Fire Safety

3. Site preparation and resistance to moisture, sub soil drainage, dangerous substances., ground moisture etc.

4. Toxic substances : relates to cavity insulation

5. Resistance to the passage of sound

6. Ventilation - particularly condensation in roofs

7. Hygiene - sanitary conveniences, hot water storage, bathroom and washing facilities

8. Drainage and Waste Disposal - foul water drainage, cesspools, septic tanks, etc.

9. Combustion appliances and fuel storage systems - air supply, discharge of combustion products from appliances

10. Protection from falling, collision and impact : stairs, ramps, ladders, vehicle barriers, etc.

11. Conservation of fuel and power

12. Access and facilities for disabled people

13. Glazing safety in relation to impact, opening and cleaning

Modern day Building Regulations, Fire Officer and Health and Safety Requirements present considerable challenges to those seeking to convert historic barns for community, business or residential use since the planners and conservation officers' requirements for sympathetic conversion retaining as much of the original fabric and character as possible will inevitably conflict with the new legal standards. Practical guidance from a building inspector well versed in such conversions is to be hoped for.

The new Localism Bill (2011) proposes significant changes to existing planning law and the transfer of more discretion over planning matters to local communities. In particular, a draft National Planning Policy Framework document has been released (August) for public consultation. It appears the general duty to preserve listed buildings and to protect and enhance conservation areas and Green Belt and farmland may be at risk when proposed Neighbourhood Plans are drawn up with related Neighbourhood Development Orders.

Regional planning is apparently to go. The intention is to impose a presumption in favour of sustainable development. The new proposals are controversial and representations have been made by the National Trust and the major heritage and conservation organisations.

Other Matters to Consider

Ensure the project is fully costed in advance of final agreement to the building contract and that prudently your bankers are reassured the financial outlays involved in conversion will be justified in terms of the estimated market value of the asset when completed. The record of conversions in practice is that many unforeseen difficulties, structural problems, timely availability of material and skilled labour (delay usually equates to increased cost) and compliance with conservation officers requirements and building regulations are each areas that can generate additional expense and without a substantial contingency reserve provision within the original costing they may jeopardise the whole project. Apart from the building contract the matters of site decontamination (e.g. leakage over long time periods of stored diesel and oils, pesticides, asbestos, fouling by stock, etc.) and final landscaping of the site will need to be brought into the overall project control and costing system. Engagement of relevant professionals such as architects specialising in the conversion of farm buildings and a separate project manager is considered advisable.

It would be prudent to ensure all professional consultants engaged on the project are adequately covered by professional indemnity Insurance (be prepared for things to go wrong and aware of whose liability the remedial cost will be).

Finally, the contractual arrangements and delineation of the development site should be drawn together by a lawyer preferably one that has a track record in these less usual conversion schemes. Additional specialist title searches should also be undertaken to flush out potential areas of unforeseen liability. It is not unknown for the presence of bats or owls in a barn to further complicate the intended conversion. In particular, a recent press article records that when builders were commencing their conversion work on a barn in

Hertfordshire a colony of bats was discovered and the local wildlife conservation officer ruled that since they were an endangered , therefore, legally protected species, they must not be removed. The problem was resolved, with client expense, by construction of a bat cave structure under the eaves sealed from the house and opened skywards by a slit to facilitate entry/exit. Bats are protected by the Wildlife and Countryside Act 1981.

The Problem of Chancel Repair Liability

High Court (March, 2000) (House of Lords, June, 2003) The case relates to a financial liability consequent upon the inheritance of a farm and land. The deeds of the land and buildings (former rectorial property) imposed on the new owner a responsibility as "lay rector" for the repair costs of a church chancel. The legal liability which originated in medieval law was confirmed by the Chancel Repairs Act, 1932, and the consequent judgement decided in favour of the parochial church council and required the landowners to pay £96,000 to repair the chancel of the 12th century St. John the Baptist Church in Aston Cantlow, Warwickshire, plus interest and legal costs. The overall liability was estimated to be in the region of £150,000 at the time of the High Court ruling (year 2000) and subsequent legal costs of appeal to the Court of Appeal and House of Lords will have added to this.

The most recent information relates to a decision of the High Court Chancery Division (The Times, 21st February, 2007) which ruled on the quantum of the liability having assessed the detailed repair schedules including VAT and the total costs including legal fees and court fees now exceed £500,000. The latest indications are that parochial church councils will be required to register chancel repair rights with the Land Registry by 2013. Purchasers of barns or other farm buildings would clearly be advised to ensure their legal representatives carry out all possible specialist searches to eliminate the unwitting purchase of land and buildings encumbered with the baggage of potentially onerous financial liabilities.

Other Liabilities

Matters that need to be considered include wayleaves for the siting of telephone poles, electricity lines, Gas or water pipelines crossing the land, also drainage ditches carrying a liability for the owner to maintain and keep clear. The question of restricted covenants is of importance. Site flood history will be an essential precaution.

The incorporation of manorial customs into the common law system may have been registered by August, 1970, under the Commons Registration Act, 1965, and thereby impose specific liabilities upon certain landowners such as the right for villagers to graze animals on the land, collect wood or, if there is a pond - to collect fish. Rights of Way across private land whilst perhaps not imposing a financial liability nevertheless intrude on privacy and should also be identified at the time of acquisition of the land and buildings. There are a number of cases where additional cost has been incurred to divert a right of way to a less intrusive part of the land. Matters of site access need also to ensure the whole access is acquired and does not expose the property purchased to "ransom strip" liabilities. Where access involves traversing common land it will be essential to seek legal rights to use this land and the local authority may grant an easement subject to a liability on the property owner to maintain the access to a particular standard. A current legal case also demonstrates the continuing existence of obscure but potentially very financially expensive legal claims over land that emanate from medieval times. The owner of the title deeds of Lord of the Manor of Hampton and Northwick in Gloucestershire is reported to be in dispute with the owners of a site in which it is claimed intended housing development would infringe certain rights bestowed on the Lord of the Manor by Royal Charter in 1331. The dispute is being referred to the High Court for a ruling. The legal costs will be significant and presumably the delay to development will also involve substantial consequential expense.

The crucial importance of seeking planning authority consent prior to commencing any work of conversion or restoration is evidenced by the law case reported in The Times, 21st March, 1995, concerning Kettleshill Oasthouse in Kent. The oast was in an advanced state of decay, and the roofs of the two roundels and barn had collapsed.

The building was heavily overgrown. The ruin was purchased in 1987 and the new owner commenced restoration work intending to use the buildings as stables. Prior planning consent had not been sought. The work proceeded to the stage where the barn roof timbers had been renewed, the roundels repaired up to roof level, the site cleared and timber for the rebuilding of the roundels roofs assembled on site. The local authority issued an enforcement notice in 1989 ordering the work to cease and all work completed was to be taken down i.e. to return the buildings to their ruined state. The owner appealed and won his case but only so far as to let the existing works remain as they were. The quality of the work was apparently not in dispute.

The owner recommenced the building works without planning permission and completed all the roof repairs and the roundels were topped off with proper cowls. In 1992, the local authority ordered all work to cease and issued an enforcement order requiring the works to be taken down. The owner appealed against the enforcement order but failed at the subsequent planning enquiry. The case was referred to the Court of Appeal and the local authority won its case against the owner who by this time had incurred considerable expense not only in terms of the actual acquisition and building works and materials but also in legal costs and court costs incurred. The costs of "taking down" will also impact upon the owner.

The owner sought leave to appeal to the House of Lords but this was refused. In 1995 the local authority ordered the owner to take down all the repairs and renovation works. The question of a final appeal to the European Courts was under consideration invoking the principle of human rights.

A further case of interest was published in The Times Law Reports dated the 9th February, 2010 and the 8th April 2011. A developer purchased 22 acres of open land in the green belt near Potters Bar in July, 1999 and applied to the local planning authority for consent to construct a barn. In December 2001 Welwyn Hatfield Council granted planning permission, subject to the condition the barn was only to be used for the storage of hay, straw or other agricultural products and not for any commercial or non-agricultural storage purposes. A building costing some £500,000 with the external appearance of a barn was constructed on the site but concealed within the frame was a two-storey, three bedroom house with reception rooms, bathroon and garage. It was connected to mains electricity, water supply and drainage and had a telephone line. All this had taken place without planning consent. In August 2002, the "barn" was occupied as a family home and in August 2006 the developer applied to the planning authority seeking a certificate of lawful use of the building as a dwelling under Section 191 of the Town and Country Planning Act 1990. In brief, this states a certificate of lawfulness is to be granted to homeowners who have lived in an unauthorised property for more than four years even if they had failed to obtain planning permission.

Welwyn Hatfield Council declined to issue a certificate and sought to bring enforcement proceedings. The case was referred to the Court of Appeal which in January 2010 ruled in favour of the developer i.e. the illegal use had continued for over four years therefore the planning authority was obliged to issue a certificate of lawful use. The case was subsequently referred to the Supreme Court and judgement given on the 6th April 2011, overturned the decision of the Court of Appeal in particular because of the original intentional and continuing deception by the developer and consequent financial advantage that would accrue to him if the certificate was allowed. The planning authority is now considering enforcement action.

Caveat Emptor

Appendix A

Boxley Abbey barn

The Cistercian Abbey at Boxley near Maidstone in Kent was founded in 1146. The destruction associated with the dissolution of the monasteries in 1538, however, left the Abbey a virtual ruin and today very little of the original buildings remain. The enclosing stone walls are substantially intact including part of the arched entrance gateway and some parts of the stone walls of the church. The present house was built in the early 18th century and the whole site including the barn remains in private ownership.

The Abbey barn dates from circa 1280 and is set within the walled grounds of the ruined Abbey. It is situated on an east/west axis and is 198ft. long. There are no aisles and stone walls carry the full weight of the barn roof yet they are without buttresses. Three entrances are set into the barn walls, there is no canopy or porch. Massive tie beams across the width of the barn are supported on the wall plates and the roof has an impressive scissor truss for some two-thirds of its length with a series of five king posts to the eastern end. A first floor level was inserted mid way with an access by stairway from the western end of the barn.

The gabled roof is covered with Kent peg tiles which were replaced following the severe storms in 1987 with grant aid from English Heritage. Sadly two large areas of these tiles are now missing/stolen. Vandals have a relatively easy access across a field from the nearby lane. It is a very exposed site and security is difficult without great expense.

PLATE 93. **Boxley Abbey Barn**
South side elevation of stone barn

Consideration is being given to various options to bring the barn back into a useful life. A rough guideline suggests a sum of about £1m. is likely to be needed to conserve and repair the barn but in the current economic climate this sum is unlikely to be forthcoming.

PLATE 94: **Boxley Abbey Barn**
North side elevation looking to the west

PLATE 95: **Boxley Abbey Barn**
North side elevation looking to the east

PLATE 96: **Boxley Abbey Barn**
West gable end

PLATE 97: **Boxley Abbey Barn**
Scissor truss roof

PLATE 98: **Boxley Abbey Barn**
Scissor truss roof

PLATE 99: **Boxley Abbey Barn**
King posts

Faversham Abbey Farm Barns, Kent

Faversham Abbey was founded in 1147 by King Stephen and Queen Matilda and was of the Benedictine Order. It was demolished at the dissolution in 1538 and much of the masonry was shipped away. The site contains a number of buildings of which the two Abbey Farm barns are the most substantial remaining structures of Faversham Abbey.

The Major Barn is set on a north-south axis. It is timber framed and aisled having weatherboard cladding and a tiled roof. The barn sits on a brick plinth and is 132ft. long and 40ft. wide with six full bays. The cart entrance with hipped roof was added in the early 19th century. The cavernous nature of the barn will be evident from the following illustrations. The aisle posts are stiffened by a long brace or shore which rises from the outer end of the aisle sill up to the head of the post being trenched (halved) into the aisle tie beam which it passes. The roof has chamfered crown posts which support the collar purlin. Some timbers have been dated to circa 1426 but most were apparently felled some fifty years later in 1475 which is the suggested date for this barn. The barn is listed Grade II star.

The Minor Barn is 40ft. wide and 86ft. long. It was originally the longer of the two barns but two or three of its bays to the eastern end were lost in the late nineteenth century. It is a timber framed aisled structure with weatherboard cladding and tiled roof . It sits upon a stone plinth. The barn has five bays and the tie beams are set over the arcade plates in normal assembly. The jowled arcade posts are stiffened at their tops by shores and braced to both the tie beam and arcade plate. The roof has five chamfered crown posts which support the collar purlin, and is said to have a complete set of original rafters. The central hipped roof cart entrance was added in the 18th century. A particularlyinteresting feature of this barn is the use of unshaped and untrimmed tree trunks as aisle posts (see illustration). Dendrochronology dating indicates a construction date of circa 1426. This barn has been listed Grade I.

The two barns were part of a working farm until some twenty years ago when they fell into disuse and suffered from neglect until being purchased by a private buyer for use as joinery workshops.

PLATE 100: **Faversham Abbey Farm Barns, Kent**

Major and Minor Barns

Appendix A | 239

PLATE 101a: **Faversham Abbey Farm Barns, Kent. Major Barn**
Timber framed and aisled (15th century)

PLATE 101b: **Faversham Abbey Farm Barns, Kent. Major Barn**
Principal posts, tie beams and plate in normal assembly

PLATE 102: **Faversham Abbey Farm Barns, Kent. Minor Barn**
Timber framed and aisled (15th century)

PLATE 103: **Faversham Abbey Farm Barns, Kent. Minor Barn**
Unshaped principal post

Appendix A | 241

PLATE 104: **Faversham: The King's Warehouse**
Octagonal crown post with head bracing

The King's Warehouse

This is a quite separate timber framed and close studded building which is of great interest. It stands on Faversham town quay and was constructed by the Corporation of Faversham in circa 1475 to provide storage facilities for local merchants and it housed the Common Beam which was a large balance for weighing heavy goods. The building was subsequently used by a ships' chandler and for sail making to service the sailing barges which used the creek. The building was carefully restored some thirty years ago and the decayed sole plates replaced. It is now occupied by the Faversham Sea Cadets.

The roof of the jettied building has octagonal and plain crown posts which support the collar purlin. Some of the posts are head braced to the purlin and collar beam and one has curved braced supports from the tie beam.

PLATE 105a: **The King's Warehouse**
Timber framed (15th century)

PLATE 105b: **The King's Warehouse**
Plain crown post supported by arch bracing from the tie beam

Appendix B

The Glastonbury Abbey barns in Somerset

The essay by C. J. Bond and J. B. Weller (see Bibliography) provides an analysis of the former Somerset barns and monastic estates of Glastonbury Abbey and includes technical descriptions and plans of each of the four surviving barns. The following comments draw upon that essay and publications by P. Rahtz and C. Platt.

The Benedictine Abbey at Glastonbury was from an early date endowed with extensive estates which provided essential support for the Abbey including its lay members through the arable produce and other revenues from the monastic farms and also from services and rents from tenants and tithes and other income from appropriated churches. In 1086 (Domesday) it is described as the richest monastery in England. By the late 13th century evidence from estate accounts for building repairs indicate that fifteen barns existed on the Abbey estates in Somerset with some locations having more than one barn. Of the four barns that remain today those at Doulting and West Pennard/West Bradley are in agricultural use, the Glastonbury Abbey barn is part of the Somerset Rural Life Museum . Pilton lacks a roof and continues to be unused.

Estimated dates for the construction of the existing buildings appear to be late 14th century. Dendrochronology examination of fifteen samples from the Glastonbury barn roof timbers indicate felling dates of 1343 - 1361. (M. Bridge, Portsmouth Polytechnic) .

Some evidence exists for an earlier date for Doulting in particular, the Abbey received licence to appropriate Doulting church in 1266 including the tithes and this may have been an incentive to invest in a new barn. The balance of views, however, puts construction at a mid fourteenth century date.

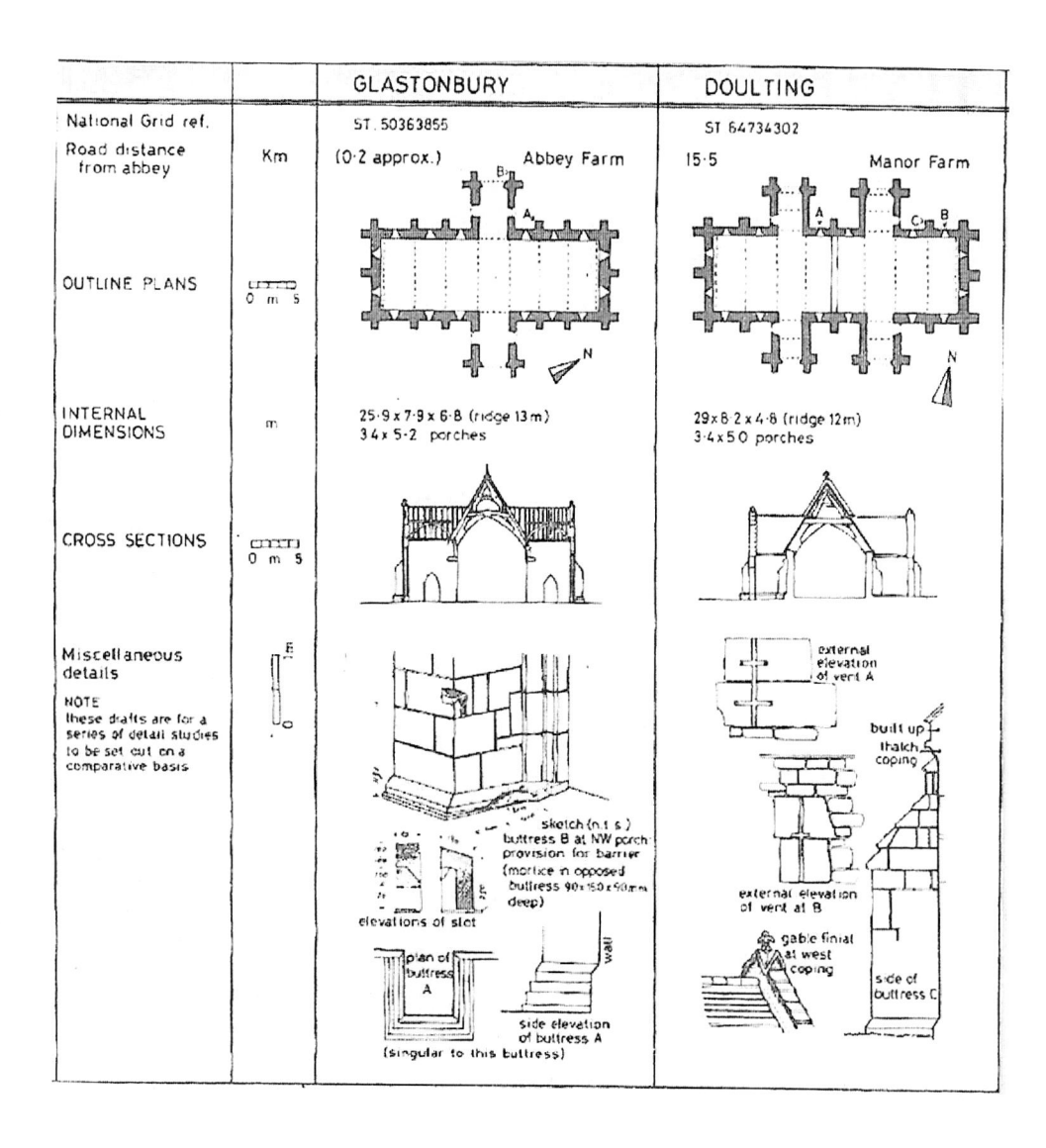

PLATE 106: **Glastonbury Abbey Barns**
Outline plans of the four barns with cross sections of each

Appendix B | 247

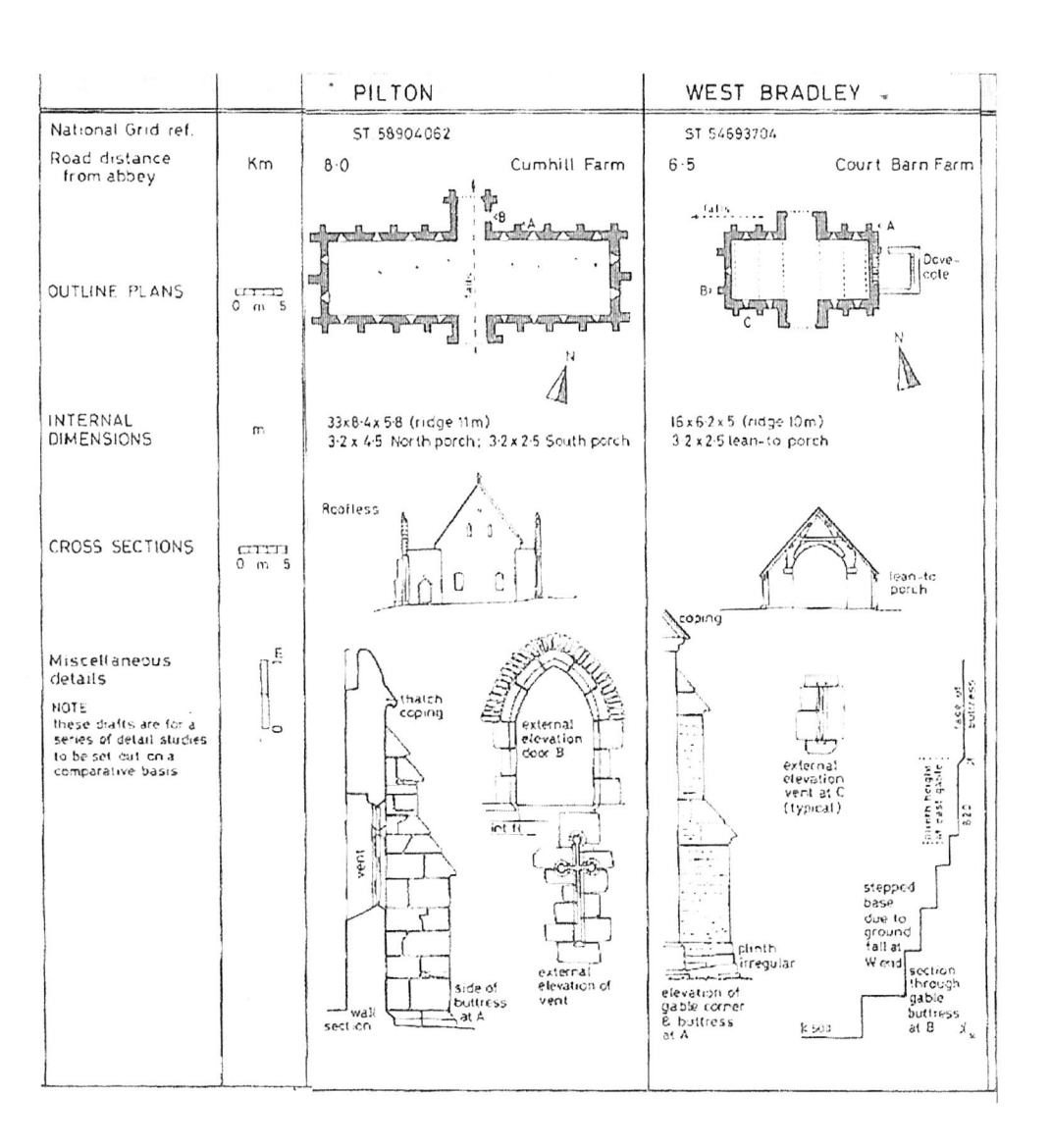

		PILTON	WEST BRADLEY
National Grid ref.		ST 58904062	ST 54693704
Road distance from abbey	Km	8·0 Cumhill Farm	6·5 Court Barn Farm
OUTLINE PLANS	0 m 5		
INTERNAL DIMENSIONS	m	33 x 8·4 x 5·8 (ridge 11m) 3·2 x 4·5 North porch; 3·2 x 2·5 South porch	16 x 6·2 x 5 (ridge 10m) 3·2 x 2·5 lean-to porch
CROSS SECTIONS	0 m 5	Roofless	lean-to porch
Miscellaneous details NOTE these drafts are for a series of detail studies to be set out on a comparative basis		thatch coping external elevation door B int fc vent side of buttress at A wall section external elevation of vent	coping external elevation vent at C (typical) plinth irregular elevation of gable corner & buttress at A stepped base due to ground fall at W end section through gable buttress at B

PLATE 106: **Glastonbury Abbey Barns**
Outline plans of the four barns with cross sections of each

Glastonbury Abbey barn is the principal barn being centrally located near to the Abbey and it displays exceptional workmanship with fine masonry. The walls are of coursed limestone rubble with bands of marlstone. Tiered buttresses, window surrounds, voussoirs and ornamentation are of high quality grey Jurassic limestone ashlar. The roof covering is of graduated stone tiles weighing in total some 80 tonnes (P. Rahtz). New roofs were built for the porches in 1976-7 being constructed as replicas of the original and several cruck blades were also replaced at that time. The common rafters are separated at their apex by a ridge purlin, originally each pair of rafters would have been secured by a side lapped joint.

Doulting barn is 96ft. long (internal) and built of Doulting stone which is a coarse grained limestone. The roof covering is of graduated stone slates and was carried on nine arch braced raised crucks but not all of these remain. A wall has been inserted dividing the internal space of eight bays equally. Because of its plainer masonry and more massive character Doulting is thought to pre-date the other three barns and it has been suggested it could well have been built soon after the acquisition of Doulting church in 1266.

Pilton barn is 108ft, long. It is built of fine quality masonry and informed opinion suggests it was probably constructed by the same masons who built the Glastonbury barn. The barn is aligned roughly east to west and has nine bays and a single gabled porch protruding midstrey on both side elevations. The stonework is coursed Liassic rubble with limestone ashlar buttresses and dressings. Ornamentation includes carvings of the four evangelists one each on the end gables and the two porch gables. The roof was destroyed by fire in 1963 and the barn remains unused. The former roof carpentry comprised ten principal trusses, raised base crucks, arch braced to the tie beam and eight intermediate mid bay trusses. A date of 1375 has been attributed to this barn.

West Pennard/West Bradley Court Barn

This is the smallest of the four barns having only five bays. It measures 53 ft. by 20 ft. with a ridge height of 33 ft. The roof structure comprised six arch braced raised base crucks of which only four remain. The roof was retiled by The National Trust with red clay tiles in the 1930's, the original roof being of stone tiles. Attached to the eastern end of the barn are the remains of a dovecote. A late 14th century date is attributed to Court Barn.

Appendix C

Survey of barns in England and Wales

In 1984 The Society for the Protection of Ancient Buildings (SPAB), in the absence of readily available quantitative information on old farm buildings, resolved to undertake a survey of all traditional barns in England and Wales (listed or not) in order to create a data base recording what barns existed, their location, type of structure, general condition and current use. Evidence over many years, particularly the number of listed building applications seeking to demolish historic barns or convert them for non traditional uses, had given rise to an increasing concern over the loss of this important aspect of heritage.

Without detailed information of what remained effective policy guidelines for its future protection would have been difficult to determine. SPAB had earlier focused media attention upon this growing dilemma by promoting a Barns Conference held at Lains Barn, Wantage, Oxfordshire in September, 1980. The conference proved successful in attracting government officials from the Ministry of Agriculture, planners, architects and media. SPAB subsequently published its Barns book in 1982 incorporating the presentations made at the earlier conference and later, exhibitions were held at various large agricultural shows.

The survey project was launched in 1984 by a special Barns Committee set up by SPAB. The scale of the survey meant it had to be co-ordinated through a network of county organisers supported by relevant societies and local groups. A public appeal for hundreds of volunteers was successful and data was gathered on a parish by parish basis using a "tick box" questionnaire. Co-operation by farmers was essential and they clearly responded well. SPAB offered advice on sources of grant aid, alternative uses for farm buildings and advice on repair methods and conversion issues. The analysed results of the survey were presented at a conference in Oxford in 1988. It was said to be the largest ever survey of farm buildings in the country, some 9136 forms had been returned and analysed and this new database, amongst other things, provided essential detail for the framing of aspects of future agricultural and rural planning policy, in particular grant aid for farm building repairs.

In 2009 English Heritage published the results of its farm buildings research project which indicated that the number of converted barns rose by 39% between 1998 and 2003. By the end of 2009, some 29,000 barns in England had been given a new use of which over 96% were residential.

Appendix D Carpentry Joints

PLATE 107a: **Carpentry joints**
Notched collar beam clasping purlin to rafter with queen post support

PLATE 107b: **Carpentry joints**
Queen strut from tie beam clasps purlin to rafter - no collar beam

PLATE 108: Carpentry joints
Stop splayed scarf joint - extends wall plate

PLATE 109: Carpentry joints
Oak dowels secure rafters at the apex of porch roof

PLATE 110: **Carpentry joints**
Solid knee brace from post to bridging beam into which the joists are set

PLATE 111: **Sussex cowl**
flat top (cap) similar to the Kent cowl but with a reduced and hooded opening

Timber-Framed Buildings of England

apex joint to rafters

lap joint between collar and rafter

collar purlin

crown post

wall plate

tie-beam

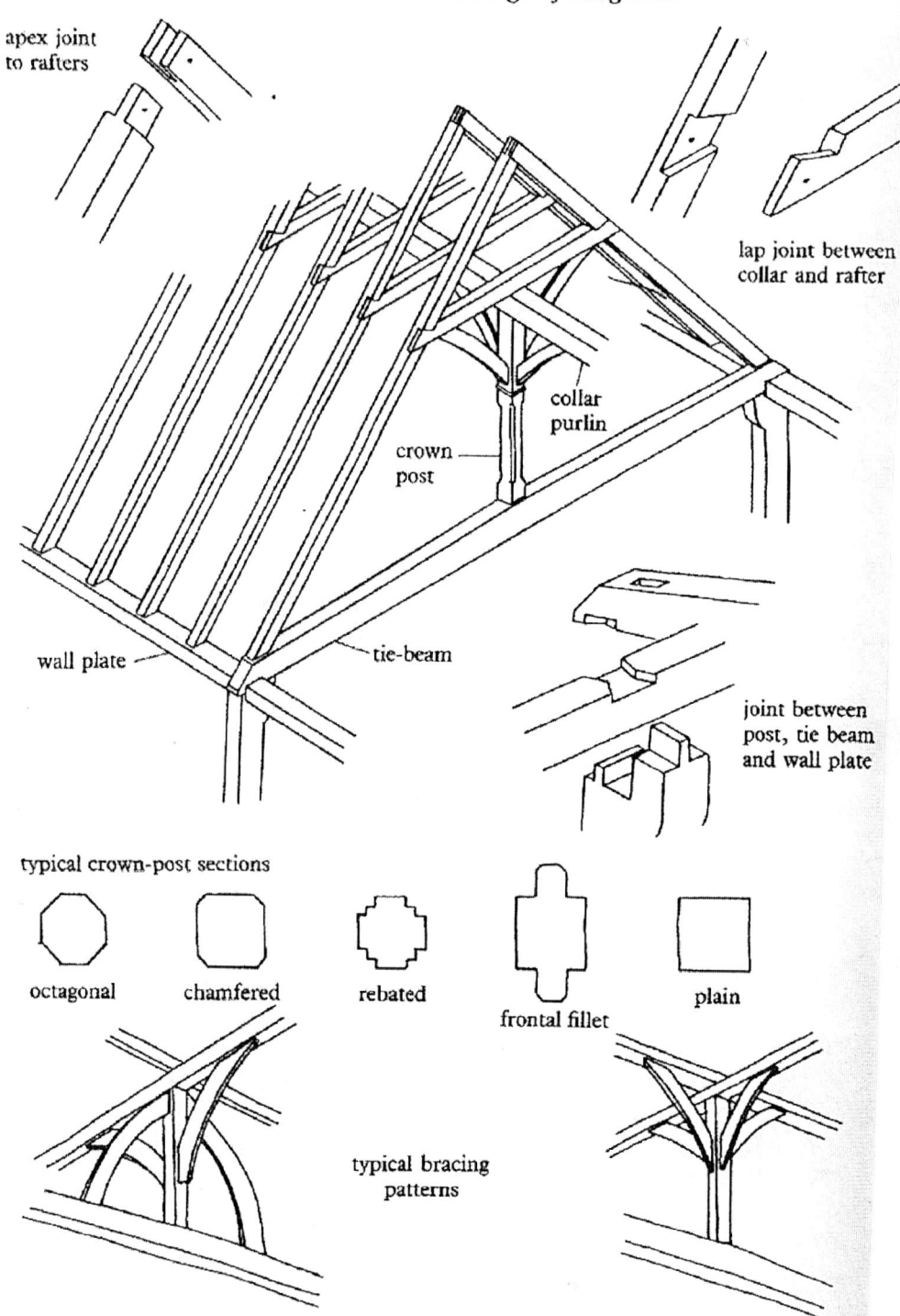

joint between post, tie beam and wall plate

typical crown-post sections

octagonal

chamfered

rebated

frontal fillet

plain

typical bracing patterns

PLATE 112: Diagrams of crown post roofs

Main References

Chapter One

Farm Statistics :
English Heritage "Living Buildings in a Living Landscape"

Definitions :
Monastic Grange Barns and the Tithe Barn - Oxford English Dictionary

Timber Framed Barns : Structural Features

R. Brunskill	Timber Building in Britain Traditional Farm Buildings in Britain
R. Brown	Timber Framed Buildings of England
J. Lake	Historic Farm Buildings
R. Harris	Discovering Timber Framed Buildings
S. Rigold	Some Major Kentish Timber Barns
F. Charles	Medieval Cruck Building and its Derivatives The Medieval Timber Framed Tradition
C. Hewett	English Historic Carpentry
J. Newlands	The Carpenter's Assistant

Rural Life in the Later Middle Ages
Castles
B. O'Neil   An Introduction to the Castles of England and Wales

C. Platt   Medieval England (p. 4 -19)

S. Sharma   A History of Britain to 1603 (p. 73, 77, 97, 107/109 and 193/194)

Late Medieval Agriculture

A. Smith   An Economic Geography of Britain (p. 3 - 33, 69 - 76 and 136 - 141)

H. Heaton   An Economic History of Europe (p. 86 - 107 and 114 -121)

E. M. Carus - Wilson   Essays in Economic History (M. Postan, Lord Beveridge, T. Bishop, E. Carus - Wilson)

S. Sharma   A History of Britain to 1603 (p. 124, 228/9, and 235/6)

Refer to the Bibliography for further references concerning this wide-ranging section that sets the barn in the context of rural life of the late Middle Ages, outlines the nature of town and village life and the craft and trade guilds and illustrates the predominance of a subsistence form of agriculture for the majority of the population.

Monastic Life

M. Aston   Monasteries

J. Dickinson   Monastic Life in Medieval England

Population Trends

B. Mitchell   British Historical Statistics

P. Morgan   Domesday Book (Kent)

C. Dyer	Making a Living in the Middle Ages (p. 5, 26, 100, 188, 234/5, 265, 300 - 303)
H. Darby	Domesday England (p. 57/63, 74, 87/89, 303/5, 337/9)
S. Sharma	A History of Britain to 1603 (p. 124, 127, 228/229, 235/6, and 369)

Medieval Building Methods

L. Salzman	Buildings in England Down to 1540
J. Harvey	The Medieval Craftsman
F. Andrews	The Medieval Builder and His Methods
G. Binding	Medieval Building Techniques

Annotated Barns Schedule

Many of the timber-framed barns have been subject to considerable changes since their original construction. In particular, raising structures onto brick or stone plinths, re-roofing including timbers and coverings, many structural timbers being replaced including recycling of timbers from other buildings, porches enlarged or new ones added, extensions made or bays reduced. Over the years, many barns suffered neglect, vandalism, serious fire or storm damage. Costly conservation work has thankfully rescued some of the best of the barn structures. Barn information and dimensions have been sourced from a wide variety of books, pamphlets and site visits over a period of time but may not be fully representative of the barns that currently exist.

Chapter Two

Methods of Dating Timber Framed Barns

C. Hewett	English Historic Carpentry (in particular p. 263 to 292) Chronology of scarf joints, post head joints, lap joints and floor framing
R. Berger	Scientific Methods in Medieval Archaeology Papers on radiocarbon dating by W. Libby, W. Horn, R. Berger, J. Fletcher, H. Suess, D. Gray and B. Damon
	Papers on dendrochronology by C. Ferguson, B. Huber and V. Giertz
P. Mellars	Article on dendrochronology - Nature, February, 2006
McGraw-Hill	Encyclopaedia of Science and Technology - entries on radiocarbon dating and dendrochronology
Britannica	Entry on carbon 14 dating

Chapter Three

The Kent Oasthouse

G. Clinch	English Hops - A History of Cultivation and Preparation for the Market from the Earliest Times
	Good general background reference including information on Reynoldes Scott and the sixteenth century oast buildings
R. Walton	Beltring Hop Farm Oasts in Kent Sixteenth to the Twentieth Century
G. Jones and J. Bell	Oasthouses in Sussex and Kent - Their History and Development
	(particularly p. 3/5, 10/14, 20/22)
R. Church	Kent - general background

Many site visits have been undertaken to survey particular oasthouse structures and useful information retrieved from exhibition displays at particular venues

Chapter Four

Barns and Oasts - Brickwork and Decorative Features

The Brickwork Development Association - Guide to Successful Brickwork

R. Brunskill   Brick Building in Britain

L. Salzman   Buildings in England Down to 1540 (p.140 /149)

Chapter Five

The Problem of Redundant Barn Structures - Planning and Legal Issues

English Heritage -   Living Buildings in a Living Landscape
    The Conversion of Traditional Farm Buildings

Planning Acts and Building Regulations

The Times Law Reports

Bibliography

1. Cecil A Hewett — English Historic Carpentry (Phillimore 1980)
2. James Newlands — The Carpenter's Assistant (Studio Editions 1990)
3. David J. Swindells — Restoring Timber-framed Houses (David & Charles 1987)
4. Graham Hughes — Barns of Rural Britain (The Herbert Press 1985)
5. Annabelle Hughes and David Johnson — West Sussex Barns and Farm Buildings Dovecote Press 2002
6. Gwen Jones and John Bell — Oast Houses in Sussex and Kent Their History and Development (Phillimore 1992)
7. Robin A. E. Walton — Oasts in Kent 16th - 20th Century. Their Construction and Equipment (Christine Swift 1985)
8. Jeremy Lake — Historic Farm Buildings (Blandford Press 1989)
9. The Brick Development Association — Guide to Successful Brickwork 2nd Edition (Butterworth Heinemann 2003)
10. Sarah Pearson — The Archbishop's Palace at Charing in the Middle Ages (2001) Archaeologia Cantiana Volume CXXI
11. R.W. Brunskill — Timber Building in Britain (London, Victor Gollancz Ltd. In Association with Peter Crawley 1985)
12. R. Brown — Timber Framed Buildings of England (Robert Hale Ltd., Clerkenwell House, Clerkenwell Green, London EC1R 0HT 1997)
13. M. Aston — Monasteries (B.T. Batsford Ltd., 4, Fitzharding Street, London W1H OAH 1993)

14.	R.W. Brunskill	Illustrated Handbook of Vernacular Architecture (Faber and Faber 1987)
15.	J. T. Smith and E. M. Yates	On the dating of English Houses from External Evidence (Field Studies Vol. 2 No. 5 1968) E. W. Classey, ltd., Hampton, Middlesex
16.	R. W. Brunskill	Brick Building in Britain (Victor Gollancz c1997)
17.	R. W. Brunskill	Traditional Farm Buildings in Britain (V. Gollancz, 1987)
18.	Rainer Berger	Scientific Methods in Mediaeval Archaeology (University of California Press 1970)
		Willard F. Libby : The Physical Science of Radiocarbon Dating
		W. Horn : The Potential and Limitations of Radiocarbon Dating in the Middle Ages - The Art Historian's View
		Rainer Berger : The Potential and Limitations of Radiocarbon Dating in the Middle Ages - The Radiochronologist's View
		J. M. Fletcher : Radiocarbon Dating of Medieval Timber Framed Cruck Cottages
		Hans E./ Suess : Climate and Radiocarbon During the Middle Ages
		D. C. Grey and P. E. Damon : Sunspots and Radiocarbon Dating in the Midddle Ages.
		C. W. Ferguson : Concepts and Techniques of Dendrochronology
		B. Huber and V. Giertz : Central European Dendrochronology for the Middle Ages
		F. W. B. Charles : The Medieval Timber Framed Tradition
		J. T .Smith : The Reliability of Typological Dating of Medieval English Roofs
19.	S. E. Rigold	Some Major Kentish Timber Barns (Archaeologica Cantiana LXXX1 - 1966)
20.	S. Sharma	A History of Britain to 1603 (BBC Worldwide Ltd. 2001)
21	W. Smith	An Economic Geography of Great Britain (Methuen And Co. Ltd.1953) p.3-33, p. 69-76, p. 136-141)

Bibliography

22.	G. F. Beaumont	A History of Coggeshall (Marshall Bros, Paternoster Row, London (1890)
		Edwin Potter, Market End, Coggeshall Press, Essex)
23.	Christopher Dyer	Everyday Life in Medieval England (Hambledon Press, 1994
24.	Edmund King	Medieval England from Hastings to Bosworth Tempus Publishing Ltd. 2005
25.	Philip Morgan	Domesday Book (KENT) Phillimore, Chichester, 1983
26.	J. C. Dickinson	Monastic Life in Medieval England A. and C. Black 1961
27.	B. R. Mitchell	British Historical Statistics (Cambridge University Press 1988)
28.	F.W. B. Charles	Medieval Cruck Buildings and its Derivatives Monograph Series (London 1967) No. 2
29,	Richard Harris	Discovering Timber Framed Buildings Shire Publications 1993 (Third Edition)
30.	B. H. St. J. O'Neil	Castles : An Introduction to the Castles of England and Wales (HMSO 1953)
31.	Colin Platt	Medieval England : A Social History and Archaeology from the Conquest to 1600 A.D. Routledge (Taylor and Francis Group 2001)
32.	Gunther Binding	Medieval Building Techniques Tempus Publishing Ltd. 2004
33.	Robin Walton	Whitbread - Beltring Hop Farm Christine Swift, Egerton, Kent. 2002
34.	Theo Barker	Shepherd Neame - A Story that has been Brewing for 300 years Granta Editions, Cambridge 1998
35.	George Clinch	English Hops - A History of Cultivation and Preparation for the Market from the Earliest Times. McCorquodale and Co. Ltd., London 1919
36.	English Heritage	The Conversion of Traditional Farm Buildings 2006
37.	English Heritage	Living Buildings in a Living Landscape (Finding a Future for Traditional farm buildings) 2006
38.	Society for the Protection of Ancient Buildings	Collection of Learned Papers Presented at (SPAB) Barns (SPAB) Conference in 1982 (The Barns Book)

39.	P. Mellars	Nature, February, 2006 (Dendrochronology) - Department Of Archaeology Cambridge University
40.	Francis B. Andrews	The Mediaeval Builder and his Methods E. P. Publishing Ltd. : Rowman and Littlefield, 1974
41	John Harvey	The Mediaeval Craftsman B. T. Batsford Ltd. London and Sydney 1975
42.	L. F. Salzman	Buildings in England Down to 1540 Oxford University Press, 1967
43.	J. Bronowski	The Ascent of Man BBC Publishing 1974
44.	R. Church	Kent Robert Hale Ltd., London WC1, 1948
45.	G. N. Gormonsway	The Anglo Saxon Chronicle J. M. Dent and Sons, Ltd. 1953
46.	G. Salusbury-Jones	Street Life in Medieval England Harvester Press Ltd. Sussex. 1975.
47.	Revd. E. L. Cutts	Parish Priests and Their People in the Middle Ages in England 1914.
48.	Abbot F. A. Gasquet	Parish Life in Medieval England Methuen and Co. 1906.
49.	Revd. H. W. Clarke	History of Tithes Swan Sonnenschein and Co. London (1894)
50.	M. Kirk	The Barn (Silent Spaces) Thames and Hudson Ltd., London (1994)
51.	Mary Gryspeerdt	Glastonbury Abbey Barn Somerset County Council Museum Service
52.	McGraw-Hill	Encyclopaedia of Science and Technology
53.		Encyclopaedia Britannica
54.	H. Heaton	Economic History of Europe Harper and Brothers, NewYork, 1948
55.	E. M. Carus-Wilson	Essays in Economic History Edward Arnold (Publishers) Ltd. London 1958
56.	H. Darby	Domesday England Cambridge University Press (1977)
57.	E.. Harris, J. Harris and N. D. G. James	Oak - A British History, Windgather Press, 2003
58.	M. Stocker	Kentish Ragstone M. Stocker, 2007

59.	K. Wilson and D. J. . White	The Anatomy of Wood, Stobart and Son, 1986
60.	D & B Martin	Historic Buildings in Eastern Sussex Vol.3 Old Farm Buildings 1450-1750

61 The Archaeology and History of Glastonbury Abbey : Collection of Essays. Edited by Lesley Abrams and James P. Carley. The Boydell Press, 1991, Essay by C. J. Bond and J. B. Weller - The Somerset Barns of Glastonbury Abbey page 57 - 87.

62 Historic Farm Buildings by Susanna Wade Martins. B. T. Batsford 1991.

63 The Village Carpenter by W. Rose. Stobart Davies Ltd. 2009.

64 English Heritage Book of Glastonbury by Philip Rahtz. B. T. Batsford Ltd. 1993.

65 The Monastic Grange in Medieval England by Colin Platt. London 1969.

66 The Cruck Built Barn of Frocester Court Farm, Glos. The Journal of the Society of Architectural Historians No. 42(1983), p.211 - 37. Article by Charles and Horn.

67 The Cruck Built Barn of Middle Littleton in Worcestershire. Journal of the Society of Architectural Historians No. 25 (1966) p. 221 - 39. Article by Charles and Horn.

68 The Cruck Built Barn of Leigh Court in Worcestershire. Journal of the Society of Architectural Historians No. 32(1973) p. 5 - 29. Article by Horn and Charles.

69 Accelerating Carbon Dating. Article by R.E.M. Hedges and J.A.J. Gowlett. Nature. March 1984.

70 New Radiocarbon Dating System. Article by Roy Switsur. Nature, Nov. 1986.

Reflections

This book presents an overview of the plight of some grand old farm buildings, namely the barn and the oast. It addresses an historic context to reflect some measure of life during the medieval period in which many of the barns were constructed and celebrates the evident skills and craftsmanship of all those involved especially the masons and carpenters. Great barns are unquestionably visually majestic structures often standing in dignified isolation within the landscape yet so clearly at one with it. Their timbers echo the rhythm of mathematics with an expression of mechanics in their geometric form. Through the many illustrations we glorify the structural beauty and visual splendour of both barn and oast, qualities often missing in our modern built environment. When abandoned, left derelict or vandalised they present a sad forlorn sight. This cannot be their fate. We should treasure our heritage. It allows a perception of what once was and is clearly worth protecting. Perhaps readers will endorse my sentiment and agree these farm buildings are deserving of preservation to provide a bridge to the past for those who follow us tomorrow.

INDEX

BARNS

Abbotsbury	18, 48, 71
Alciston	71
Avebury	75,77-79, 80
Aylesford Priory	22 74,81-86
Aylton Court Farm	28
Ashleworth	72
Abbey Farm, Norfolk	74
Abbey Farm, Snape, Suffolk	75
Brook, Wye, Kent	73
Bishop's Barn. Wells	74
Bradford on Avon	20,32,75,87-91
Buckland Abbey	48,71
Bredon	73
Boxley, Kent	73& Appdx. A
Carlisle, St. Mary's	26,71
Caldicote, Herts.	66
Cressing Temple	18,20,30,32,72, 122-126,147, 214,215
Coggeshall	4,32,72,112-115
Charing, Kent	73,132-134
Copdock, Ipswich	75,211,214
Chiddingley, East Sussex	211,213
Doulting, Somerset	74,92,93&Appdx. B
Exceat, Sussex	30,71,135-137
Falmer	71
Farnham	66
Faversham, Kent	Appdx.A
Frindsbury	18,21,22,24,30,73,127-131
Felsted	28
Frocester	72
Glastonbury	32,75,94-98,Appdx.B
Great Dixter	21,72,109-111
Great Coxwell	22,30,74,99-103
Hales, Norfolk	18,74,214
Harmondsworth	65,74
Leigh Court	73
Littlebourne	18,19,21,22,73,104-108
Leiston Abbey, Suffolk	75
Little Bromley, Essex	49
Middle Littleton	73
Mote Farm, Kent	192
Old Basing, Hants.	72
Ormesby, Norfolk	64
Paul's Hall Barn, Essex	147
Pilton, Somerset	74
Penshurst, Kent	66
Preston Plucknett, Somerset	74
Scotney Castle Estate	22,23,182-184
Sissinghurst	32,73,168,171
Stanton, Glos.	72
Stowmarket, Suffolk	75
Tisbury Place Farm	75
Titchfield Abbey,Hamts.	72
Torre Abbey, Devon	48,71
Uffington	66
West Pennard	75
Westenhanger, Kent	21,73,116-120
Winscombe Grange, Somerset	65
Widdington , Essex	72

OASTHOUSES

Beltring	58,164-167,209
Chartwell	160,187,188
Flimwell	158
Goudhurst	189,201
Hadlow	196
Kettleshill	228,229
Knockholt	197,211
Mote Farm	160,190-192
Museum of Kent Life	160,177-181
Scotney Castle Estate	182-186
Sissinghurst	158,168-176,207,209
Spelmonden	189,207,212
West Malling	193-195,209,212
Woodchurch	198-200,209
Hop Drying	160,162
Hop Press	163,175
Hop Statistics	155,156

OTHER MATTERS

Brick Bond and Decoration	203
Dendrochronology	147,148,149
Radiocarbon dating	145,146 147
Survey of Barns	Appdx. C
Thatch	30,31
Carpentry Joints	Appdx.D